excuses

for all occasions

excuses
for all occasions

Alibis, Apologies, and Cop-Outs
That Can Get You Out of
(or Into) Trouble

Steven D. Price

Skyhorse Publishing

Skyhorse Publishing books may be purchased in bulk at special discounts for sales promotion, corporate gifts, fund-raising, or educational purposes. Special editions can also be created to specifications. For details, contact the Special Sales Department, Skyhorse Publishing, 307 West 36th Street, 11th Floor, New York, NY 10018 or info@skyhorsepublishing.com.

Skyhorse® and Skyhorse Publishing® are registered trademarks of Skyhorse Publishing, Inc.®, a Delaware corporation.

Visit our website at www.skyhorsepublishing.com.

10 9 8 7 6 5 4 3 2 1

Library of Congress Cataloging-in-Publication Data is available on file.

ISBN: 978-1-61608-597-1

Printed in China

Contents

Excuses for All Occasions

Contents

Qui s'excuse, s'accuse [he who excuses himself accuses himself].

—French proverb

.

Introduction

Alexander Pope made a point when he wrote that "to err is human; to forgive, divine," but if anything is even more human than erring, it's finding excuses for being wrong. From the Biblical account of Eve's blaming the serpent for tempting her to eat that apple to more contemporary "the devil made me do it" utterances by contemporary politicians and celebrities who have been discovered with their fingers in the cookie jar (a metaphor for a variety of sins), the history of the world is fraught with apologies, justifications, alibis, and other expressions of innocence, regret or defensiveness.

Why the need for excuses? The primary reason is to hide or distract from a lack of competency. In our own minds, we're perfect or at least competent in every aspect of our lives, so when we fail, it's due to circumstances beyond our control or because of some sort of momentary fall from grace that we can excuse in ourselves (but woe to anyone else who says or does the same thing). In baseball, it's a fielder's "I lost it in the sun" when in fact the player misjudged the pop fly or—and this is the reason why Billy Loes most famously gave the excuse—a ground ball. In the business world, it's blaming another department or a technical glitch because a report wasn't produced on time when in fact the employee waited till the last minute and then discovered he or she didn't have sufficient data. In romance it's because he's a bastard or she's a bitch. Our fault? Were we in any way guilty of what the law calls contributory negligence? Who me? Nah, never happen.

Psychologists suggest that excuses help people rationalize in their mind why they didn't do what they should have done or, conversely, why they did do what they shouldn't have done. And because these are rationalizations, a word that has its root in "logic" or "reason," rationalizers find their excuses reasonable. Their excuses are not excuses, they are reasons. And the longer they rationalize their behavior, the more easily they see their excuses as the truth—the dog really did eat your homework even if it's an elderly Chihuahua that can barely gum down its dinner and the homework was inside a thick plastic binder.

Blaming the victim is a prime example; a physician explaining away a potential malpractice situation with; "It was the patient's fault. If he had taken better care of himself, this error wouldn't have caused so much harm." (As the old line goes, doctors bury their mistakes, lawyers visit them on a prison visiting day).

Speaking of medicine, rationalizers seem to enjoy latching on health excuses. Syndromes are a fertile field. Let's say you're accused of being unable to accept responsibility or otherwise behaving like an adult. That's not your fault, you counter—you suffer from Peter Pan Syndrome. Can't get around to cleaning up your room or office cubicle? Of course not—you suffer from tertiary Bag Lady Syndrome.

"Syndrome's" first cousin is "issues." Someone accidentally nudges your rear bumper while you're sitting in your car. You get out yelling and screaming and, even though there's no discernable damage, you threaten the driver with grievous bodily harm which you express in terms that would curdle a Marine drill instructor's blood. Are you blowing the incident out of control? Perhaps, but you can't help it because you have "anger management issues."

The more you stick to your excuse, whether or not it's a rationalization, the more readily others will be convinced. Adolf Hitler espoused the phenomenon in his infamous "Big Lie" theory: if you make up a story that's so preposterous that people can't believe that anyone would have distorted the truth to that extent, why then, what you say must be true.

Some excuses are intended to deceive but in a kindly fashion. We call them "white lies," ways to beg off an invitation to what you know will be a deadly dull dinner party with a "thank you, but I have a previous commitment." Or to discourage a nerd who's hitting on you with "Don't think that I'm not flattered by your attention, but you should know that I have a boyfriend."

Governments, which are widely known never to make mistakes, have their own brand of "agen-

Introduction

cy double-talk" excuses whereby agencies explain away mistakes in langue where, if you didn't know what really happened and why it did, you'd be quite content with such plausible denial. Take, for example, the Charge of the Light Brigade, a cavalry attack by the British against an insurmountable Russian gun battery position during the 19th-century Crimean War. Tennyson got it right when he wrote in his celebrated poem: "Forward, the Light Brigade!"/ Was there a man dismay'd?/ Not tho' the soldier knew/ Some one had blunder'd."

Yes, the Charge of the Light Brigade was a mistake: the suicidal assault happened because the brigade's commander Lord Cardigan (he of the front-buttoned sweater) either misheard orders or, as some historians argue, chose to disregard them. And how was the blunder that resulted in so many deaths explained away? "It was an unfortunate lapse by an individual which has now been dealt with under internal disciplinary procedures."

• • •

Excuses for All Occasions

Excuses for All Occasions is intended both to delight and instruct. Most of the explanations, justifications, alibis, weasel-words, and outright falsehoods that you'll find in these pages are very amusing, if not for their inventiveness then because they're beyond pathetic. You'll read some with a shock of recognition and others with a shudder that anyone in his right mind would try to get away with such foolishness . . . until you remember similar occasions of your own where desperate times of "deer-caught-in-headlights" proportions called for desperate measures.

I approached the traffic-ticket and jury-duty categories with the same attitude that I had for the others, which is to say I'd find and/or concoct wild and wool excuses of all degrees of plausibility. But then I reconsidered. Tangling with The Law is rarely a laughing matter, so I began those chapters with straightforward, sensible information about dealing with law-enforcement officers and the court system.

As with the other compendia that I've compiled, people ask which of the entries are my favorites. And

Introduction

as with my other books, there are too many good ones to single out even a handful, but if pressed, I'd have to cite the following:

President Bill Clinton's no-nonsense explanation of why he dallied with Monica Lewinisky: "Because I could."

This tax-evader's testimony to the power of prayer: "I went to a lonely road and prayed that I should become self-sufficient and be able to help others, and a short time later I received a $836,939.19 check upon my discharge from the Army. I didn't report it on my tax return because I thought the check was a miraculous answer to my prayer instead of a Government error."

This reason to stay on line: "That blonde on *College Girls On Spring Break* looks a lot like your brother's younger daughter. I'd better keep watching to make sure it isn't her."

And finally, the blue ribbon-winning, you-can't-make-that-stuff-up lollapalooza of all excuses from Zambian tennis player Lighton Ndefwayl on why he lost a match to rival Musumba Bwayla: "Musumba

Bwayla is a stupid man and a hopeless player. He has a huge nose and is crosseyed. Girls hate him. He beat me because my jockstrap was too tight and because when he serves he farts, and that made me lose my concentration, for which I am famous throughout Zambia."

Try and top that one, folks. And if you think you can or if you think you have, then, in the deathless and all-purpose phrase of comedian Steve Martin, "Well, excuuuuse me!"

Steven D. Price
New York, N.Y.
January 2012

Acknowledgement

O f the many kind friends and relatives who pointed me toward clever and preposterous and eminently repeatable excuses, including some of their own, I must thank in particular Rich Goldman, Tony Ard, Betsy Wesman, Mike Cohen, Jim Wofford, Jim Babb, John Thornton, Andrea and Mitchell Sweet, Beth Carnes and Tim Rowland, and Skyhorsemen Tony Lyons and Bill Wolfsthal.

Finally, for me not to acknowledge the assistance, ingenuity, and patience of Sara Kitchen, editor, colleague, and friend, would be thoroughly inexcusable.

"No one ever excused his way to success."

—*Dave Del Dotto*

1.

Whether it's because of all the media attention or because they've become adept at finding ways to talk their way out of sticky situations, people who are involved in politics and entertainment are prime candidates for coming up with prime excuses.

Politicians

"I didn't inhale . . . "

—*President Bill Clinton, admitting that he tried marijuana.*

"When the President does it, that means that it's not illegal."

—*President Richard M. Nixon in a television interview with journalist David Frost, justifying his actions surrounding Watergate.*

Celebrity Excuses

"[The] bitch set me up!"

>*—Washington, D.C. mayor Marion Barry,*
>*reacting to an FBI raid after the agents saw a*
>*live video of him lighting a crack pipe.*

"I apologize if my comments offended."

>*—Kentucky Senator Jim Bunning, after*
>*predicting that Supreme Court Justice Ruth*
>*Bader Ginsburg would not survive her*
>*pancreatic cancer.*

"I don't think anybody anticipated the breach of the levees."

>*—President George W. Bush, after a week of*
>*repeated warnings about the expected effect of*
>*Hurricane Katrina.*

Excuses for All Occasions

"[Michael Chertoff did not know] the first thing about running a disaster."

> —*Michael Brown, Federal Emergency Manage-*
> *ment Agency chief, blaming his superior, who*
> *was the head of the Department*
> *of Homeland Security.*

"We finally cleaned up public housing in New Orleans. We couldn't do it, but God did."

> —*Louisiana Congressman Richard Baker,*
> *after Hurricane Katrina.*

"Harry Whittington didn't 'announce himself.'"

> —*Katharine Armstrong, owner of the ranch on*
> *which Vice President Dick Cheney shot his*
> *hunting companion while quail hunting.*

Celebrity Excuses

"I had other priorities."

> —*Dick Cheney, on why he avoided military service in Vietnam.*

"I didn't mean to say it."

> —*Roberta McCain, 95-year-old mother of presidential candidate John McCain, excusing herself for blaming Mormons for the 2002 Salt Lake City Olympics bribery scandal.*

"Al-Qaeda militants have slipped hallucinogenic pills in their coffee with milk, like Nescafé."

> —*former Libyan dictator Moammar Gadhafi, explaining why Libyan citizens were dissatisfied with his leadership.*

"I didn't learn how to be careful with my words, didn't learn how to be cautious about what we were trying to get done in ways that were self-destructive."

—Newt Gingrich, on his House of Representatives failures with regard to his communications strategy.

"*Et alors?*" ["So what?"]

—France's former president François Mitterrand, replying to a journalist about his secret illegitimate daughter whom he maintained at the state's expense.

Celebrity Excuses

"I have a Saints party . . . and I am absolutely going to be there for the big game, kickoff of the Saints and the whole NFL . . . As a fanatic (Saints fan), I have my priorities."

—Senator David Vitter of Louisiana, on why he hosted a New Orleans Saints-Green Bay Packers TV party with friends and family in Lousiana instead of attending President Barack Obama's economic address before a joint session of Congress.

"I'm not making any excuses for my behavior. I don't do drugs. I was not drinking. That wasn't the cause of this. This was me doing a dumb thing and doing it repeatedly and then lying about it. And that's all there is."

—Rep. Anthony Weiner, after being caught emailing provocative photos of himself to a woman who was not his wife

"I didn't say that I didn't say it. I said that I didn't say that I said it. I want to make that very clear."

—*George Romney, automobile executive, former governor of Michigan, presidential contender, and father of Mitt Romney.*

Show Business

"[It] just slipped out. I was a little excited."

—Melissa Leo, winner of the Best Supporting Actress Oscar, explaining why she included the four-letter word that begins with "f" in her acceptance speech.

"I was told that I should shoplift, I'm doing a role where I am required to shoplift. My director said I should try it out. I probably should have notified the store and said I was going to come and shoplift. I'm sorry."

—actress Winona Ryder, after being caught shoplifting

"What I have seen of it is beautiful. I came once before to visit The Andy Warhol Museum whilst researching a film and found both the city and its inhabitants warm and gracious."

—actress Sienna Miller, after referring to the city of Pittsburg as "Shitsburg" in a Rolling Stone magazine interview.

"I can't be cool . . . I can't be laidback. It's something that has happened and I feel I want to celebrate it and I wanna celebrate her [Katie Holmes]. She's a very special woman."

—actor Tom Cruise, explaining why he jumped on the couch while being interviewed by Oprah Winfrey on her TV show.

Celebrity Excuses

"Those words were never meant to be hurtful to anyone. They were an accident of my distraction and a product of news sensationalism. I am deeply saddened by the pain that this whole situation has caused the victims of the devastating earthquake in China."

—actress Sharon Stone, after speculating that the earthquake might have been the result of karma because of the Chinese government's treatment of Tibet and the Dalai Lama.

"My daughter had a softball game I desperately wanted to go to, and I was a little impatient. I said some things I shouldn't have said."

—ex-CNN talk show host Rick Sanchez after calling The Daily Show host Jon Stewart a bigot and making racial slurs against CNN's management.

Excuses for All Occasions

" . . . a ridiculous act, the gesture of a girl rebel."

—singer Sinead O'Connor, after tearing up a photo of Pope John Paul II as she sang the word "evil" on Saturday Night Live.

"It's like I have a loaded gun in my mouth and my finger's on the trigger, and I like the taste of the gunmetal."

—actor Robert Downey Jr., describing his life, which included drug abuse and outrageous public conduct.

"Why would I put a scarf over the baby's face if I was trying to throw him off the balcony? I was kind enough to let them see. I was doing something out of innocence."

—Michael Jackson, after suspending his baby out of a hotel room window.

Celebrity Excuses

"My lawyers didn't explain what a suspended license meant."

—celebrity Paris Hilton, after being arrested for driving without a valid license.

"It was just one of those quirky, sort of naughty, sort of wild, you know, drunken things that people will do from time to time."

—actor Rob Lowe, on why he filmed himself in bed with a sixteen-year-old girl.

"An open-handed slap is justified—if all other alternatives fail and there has been plenty of warning. If a woman is a bitch, or hysterical, or bloody-minded continually, then I'd do it."

—actor Sean Connery, who also commented, "There are women who take it to the wire. That's what they are looking for, the ultimate confrontation. They want a smack."

"I feel like Madonna is using mind control over him."

—*Cynthia Rodriguez, wife of baseball star Alex Rodriguez, on his infidelity with pop star Madonna.*

"I picked her up because she needed a ride. It's not the first hooker I've helped out. I've seen hookers on corners and I'll pull over, and they'll go, 'Oh, you're Eddie Murphy, oh my God,' and I'll empty my wallet out to help."

—*movie actor Eddie Murphy, after being arrested with a transvestite prostitute.*

"I have severe acid reflux."

—*singer Ashlee Simpson, explaining she lip-synched a song on Saturday Night Live*

Celebrity Excuses

"His words were taken out of context."

—Russell Crowe's publicist, justifying Crowe's implication that actress Sharon Stone looked like a chimpanzee after she had a face-lift.

"Deep and seemingly endless frustration."

—How Alex Baldwin explained calling his 14-year-old daughter a "rude little pig." The frustration had to do with his relationship with actress Kim Basinger.

"A little acknowledgment [from supermodel wife Christie Brinkley], a little attention, a little thank-you every now and then for my efforts."

—Peter Cook, on why he had an affair with his 18-year-old assistant.

Criminals

"I didn't want to hurt them, I only wanted to kill them."

—David Berkowitz, the "Son of Sam" serial murderer who contended that a demon that controlled a neighbor's dog "Sam" had ordered him to kill.

"That fucking bitch, why didn't she leave me alone?"

—what Robert Chambers (called "the Preppie Killer" by the media) reportedly said to his father before being booked for the murder in New York's Central Park of Jennifer Levin, who he claimed wanted "rough sex."

"Wasn't mine."

—actor Tom Sizemore, after being caught with a prosthetic penis filled with drug-free urine during a drug test.

Celebrity Excuses

"These are troubled kids in a very difficult and grotesque home environment, and they cracked."

—Leslie Abramson, the attorney who defended Erik and Lyle Menendez, brothers who murdered their parents.

"I didn't show up for court, because I didn't have a professional bodyguard."

—singer Courtney Love, on failing to appear for a hearing on a drug-possession charge.

"I didn't want to, but I just thought if I didn't do it he wouldn't be my friend anymore."

—Amy Fisher, "the Long Island Lolita" imprisoned for having shot the wife of her boyfriend, Joey Buttafuoco, explaining why she had sex with a prison guard.

"I felt stressed because of the death of Michael Jackson."

—An unnamed Ohio woman, explaining why she started a fire in the bathroom of a bar.

" . . . the police, since my trouble, have not worked out for me."

—O.J. Simpson, on why he chose not to ask the Las Vegas police to help him reclaim stolen goods.

"He didn't love me and never would. I had a very hard time accepting that."

—Susan Smith, explaining why she drowned her two young children in 1994 when her boyfriend refused to marry her because she was a mother.

Celebrity Excuses

"I have dry skin, and I have to itch it a lot."

—Joseph Scordata, age 81, arrested for masturbating in his parked car. (He subsequently claimed "That's not possible . . . I don't have a penis.")

"You're lying! I should have blown your head off! . . . " If I had been the one that was there."

—a defendant representing himself in trial when the shop owner identified him as the robber.

"I was throwing the rocks to guide her back to shore."

—explanation by a husband accused by the police of throwing his wife off a bridge into West Virginia's Kanawa River. Unhurt by the fall, she swam toward the river bank, at which time the defendant hurled rocks at her.

More Celebrity Excuses

"I'm not the kind of person I'm being portrayed as . . . [I am] a good person."

—convicted financier Bernard Madoff.

"Both racial preferences and racism played a role."

—former New York Times reporter Jayson Blair, explaining why he fabricated stories at the newspaper.

"We're living in a day when one problem follows another, and when it comes to trying to recognize the truth of prophecy, we're finding it very, very difficult."

—Minister Harold Camping, explaining why his prediction that the world would come to an end on October 21, 2011, was a miscalculation. Camping has also predicted that the end of the world would occur on Sept. 6, 1994, then again on May 21, 2011.

Celebrity Excuses

Waitress: "And another thing, don't be so free with your hands."

W. C. Fields: "Listen honey. I was only trying to guess your weight."

—from the W.C. Fields classic comedy film,
Never Give a Sucker an Even Break.

"We are all manufacturers: some make good, others make trouble, and still others make excuses."

—*Anonymous*

2.

A man's home may be his castle, but it's also a fertile source of reasons not to treat it like a palace.

Not Paying the Rent

Oops, I forgot to wind my calendar.

I was away for most of the month.

I'm a little short this month—take it out of the security deposit.

The light is out in the hallway, and I'm not paying till it's fixed.

I paid last month—that should hold me for a while.

It was my roommate's turn to pay, but she's out of the country—maybe for good.

Excuses for the Home

I can't find the lease, and I can't remember what the rent is.

The front door squeaks, and the handyman won't oil it.

The doorman lost one of my packages.

The stove is a fire hazard.

The Wall Street Occupiers didn't pay rent, and they're on the side of the angels.

Something on the roof is messing up my TV reception.

The landlord owes me a paint job for two months now.

I'm saving the money for Christmas tips for the landlord and the building staff.

Not Cooking

Who has the time?

I should have let my mother teach me how . . . but I didn't.

I'm on a diet.

With schedules like ours? No way!

The dishwasher's broken.

I tried it once, and I burned myself. See . . . here's the scar.

My mother-in-law is a terrific cook. I don't want my husband comparing me to her in those terms, too.

Ramen noodles are healthy and filling, and you don't have to wash the bowl.

Excuses for the Home

I eat at the office and expense-account the charges.

Waiters and busboys are depending on me.

I can live on peanut butter and banana sandwiches.

Do I look like Rachael Ray / the Iron Chef?

I use the oven to store things.

The cookbook says the dish takes an hour to make. The order-in delivery guy will be here in 20 minutes.

If you can't get it at McDonald's, it's not worth eating.

I cooked once and chipped a finger nail.

Not Cleaning Out Rooms and Closets

It's too nice a day—let's wait for a rainy day.

It's raining—the dampness will kill my back/knee/shoulder.

All that dust will make mincemeat out of my sinuses.

The attic's too hot—let's wait till winter.

The basement (or garage) is too cold—let's wait till summer.

There are squirrels (or bats) in the attic / there are mice in the basement. What if one escapes into the house?

I promised the kids I'd take them to a ball game/the movies/the library/the mall.

Excuses for the Home

I promised the guys I'd play golf/tennis/poker/go fishing/go hunting.

Charlie is looking at new cars, and he wants my advice.

There's a big game on the tube.

I have to prepare for a big meeting/big test on Monday.

My roommate's sleeping.

The storage place is closed today.

Your mother's coming later today.

And when you can't put off the chore any longer . . .

What do you mean, throw it away? It has tremendous sentimental value.

But those magazines are a complete set.

But that belonged to my mother/father/great-uncle. I'm saving it for the kids when they grow up.

But those electric trains are not rusty—they'd work. Besides, they're collectors items.

But I'll donate those golf clubs to a worthy cause when I get around to it.

You have no sense of history.

I'll throw the albums away after I scan the photos next week. I promise.

Excuses for the Home

But that was my father's high school year-book.

I'll fit into those pants again when I lose a few pounds.

I'll use that rowing machine to lose a few pounds.

So what if a few spokes are missing?

I hear that Hula Hoops are coming back.

Soak those paintbrushes in turpentine, and they'll be as good as new.

I'll finish that birdhouse one of these days.

Someday you'll want it.

All that radio needs is a few new tunes, and it'll work fine.

Let's save it for when the kid goes off to college (or has his/her first apartment).

Leave it there—I'll ask your brother whether he wants it back.

My mother's? I thought it was *your* mother's!

Haven't you heard of the "retro" look?

If I can get the lid off, I'll show you that paint hasn't dried up.

No, I don't have too much fishing tackle! No fisherman ever has too much tackle.

Excuses for the Home

All it needs is fresh batteries, and it'll run as good as new.

But I'm planning to read that book someday.

"One of the most important tasks of a manager is to eliminate his people's excuses for failure."

—*Robert Townsend*

3.

Whoever said "if you only put as much effort into your work as you do trying to get out of it, you'd be a millionaire" just didn't understand the problem.

Not Getting a Job

I'm not a morning person.

People at my last job looked at me funny.

The holidays are coming up, and no one hires during the holidays.

I'm overqualified for most jobs.

I'll wait till the economy improves.

My family needs me to look after the house when they're all at work.

Work Excuses

I've got ten weeks of unemployment benefits left, and if I don't use them, I'll lose all the money that's coming to me.

I want to improve my communication skills first.

It's summer, and no one hires during the summer.

I'm not really a people person.

I haven't found anything that's really challenging.

I'm waiting till the kids get out of school/go back to school.

There's nothing but dead-end jobs with no hope for quick advancement to upper management.

I'm shy about using bathrooms with other people.

I'm too old.

This is my lucky lottery ticket—I feel it in my bones.

I'll wait till after the election, then look again.

Being Late for or Absent from Work

The Occupiers were protesting, and they blocked the street in front of this building.

I won't be in because of eye trouble—I can't see working today.

My smart-phone won't recharge, and I can't go anywhere without it.

Work Excuses

A neighbor has a problem. It wouldn't be neighborly not to help her.

I recently converted to Hinduism, and there was a cow in the road.

An old lady playing a computer game asked me to help her reach the next level.

I have a case of Spring Fever.

I thought I could ride my son's/daughter's bike/scooter/skateboard without hurting myself. It turns out I can't.

I'm still drunk from last night's office party.

I am extremely sensitive to the rise in interest rates.

I need a mental day.

I woke up in a strange bed, and I have no idea where I am.

Excuses for All Occasions

My car ran out of gas on the way to work, and it feels like I got a hernia pushing it to the nearest gas station.

My eyes won't open.

The city is paving my street and I can't get out of the driveway.

I spent all my money playing online bingo and I can't afford the bus. I'll try to win today while I'm home.

I have a chance of filling in for someone on jury duty.

I won't be in to work today—my brain is full.

I have to stay home—the voices told me to clean all my guns today.

I took two Ex-Lax in addition to my Prozac. I won't dare leave the bathroom, but I feel good about it.

Work Excuses

I met your [the boss's] daughter in a bar last night, and she told me, in your opinion, it would be okay to be late for work.

The radio said there could be traffic jams this morning. I didn't want to help make everybody else late for work.

The dog ate my car keys. We've got to walk to the vet.

I do not feel up to par today.

I'm having the worst bad hair day of my life.

I forgot to take in the Sunday newspaper yesterday, and by the time I had realized that today was in fact Monday, it's not worth coming in.

I spent my paycheck on lottery tickets, and I'm out of gas till payday.

The police closed down the street—there's a sniper in the neighborhood.

Excuses for All Occasions

I drove to my old office out of habit.

I just found out I'm pregnant, and I had to wait for my mother to wake up so I could call her.

I didn't think you'd notice when I came in.

My child has a cold, and my computer has a virus.

My spirit guide says work is for losers.

I'm feeling extremely lethargic today—are you sure you want me to come in?

I had to buy a lottery ticket, and the line was endless.

A skunk sprayed me, and I was all out of tomato juice.

[When you're late] Don't pay the ransom—I escaped.

Work Excuses

The drawbridge was stuck open.

I forgot to wind my watch.

I forgot to change the calendar.

A deer jumped in my swimming pool and drowned, and I have to wait till the health department comes to pull the body out.

There was a power failure in our neighborhood, and my clock radio didn't go off.

The vet said that if I don't spend quality time with my cat, she'll keep peeing on the bed.

I went to see friends off on a Caribbean cruise. The ship left with me still on it, and the captain won't turn back. I'll be back in the office next Thursday at the earliest.

My husband thinks it's funny to hide my car keys before he goes to work.

Excuses for All Occasions

I got locked in my car trunk by my son.

A gurney fell out of an ambulance and delayed traffic.

I feel like I'm in everyone's way if I show up on time.

My driveway washed away in last night's rain.

The garbage bag broke while I was putting it in the garbage can, and I got coffee grounds all over my last clean shirt and pants.

I didn't pay my electricity bill so I can't see to get ready.

I dropped my car keys in the snow, and I'm waiting for the snow to melt so I can find them.

My wife plans to become pregnant today, and I want to be there.

It was foggy, and I missed the building.

Work Excuses

My car's left-turn blinker broke, and I had to make right turns all the way to the office.

I lost my dentures while swimming in the ocean, and I have to get a new pair at the dentist.

I discovered stigmata, which makes me think I may be a likely candidate for the Second Coming.

I can't come in today as I have an interview for a job I really want and I don't want to lie to you.

I can't come to work today because I have the brown bottle flu.

I confused Martin Luther King's birthday with Elvis's. They were both King, you know.

I can't undo the knot in my shoelaces.

I'm sorry I won't be in today. I have to rescue my friends and save the world.

Excuses for All Occasions

A man drove his car into my house.

I left my work boots at work.

The hamster is loose in the house somewhere and if I don't find it and put it back in its cage before I leave, the cat will get it, and the kids will be broken-hearted.

We went across to Canada for dinner. I left my driver's license at home. The border patrol wouldn't let me back in, so my wife had to leave me at a hotel while she drove the two hours back to our house and then back to pick me up.

I took my car to a car wash after work. Water must have gotten into the door locks and they froze during the night, and I can't get the key in.

I lost my American Express Card, and they said don't leave home without it.

Work Excuses

I would have been on time, but I picked up a hitch-hiker who didn't want to be dropped off in the middle of the city, so I had to drive way out of my way to leave him at a truck stop.

[On a Friday] I can't come to work today because my father is dying.

[Followed by] I can't come to work today because my father didn't die yesterday. He's waiting till Monday.

I can't find my glasses and I need them in order to find them.

I thought Saint Patrick's Day is a paid vacation day.

I thought Daylight Savings was "Spring back, Fall ahead."

I have a headache and do not want to give it to anyone else.

Excuses for All Occasions

I contracted some attention-deficit disorder and, hey, how about them Red Sox, huh?

I just found out that I was switched at birth. Legally, I shouldn't come to work knowing my employee records now contain false information.

I converted my calendar from Julian to Gregorian.

I refuse to travel to my job until there is a commuter tax. I insist on paying my fair share.

My cat was upset by my talking in my sleep. She jumped off the bed, knocked my alarm off the dresser, the batteries fell out, and so I over-slept.

EMPLOYEE: Sorry I'm late, but I couldn't get my car started.

BOSS: Why not?

EMPLOYEE: I was asleep at the time.

When Business Projects Fail

We didn't have enough time.

The budget was unrealistic.

Too much input from the client.

Too little input from the client.

The client changed his mind a dozen times.

It was office politics as usual.

No cost control supervision.

Did you ever try dealing with foreign suppliers?

We inherited a can of worms from the former team.

Someone forgot to inform the client that it was the beta version.

The team was shorthanded.

The test groups couldn't agree on anything.

The balance sheet was out of whack.

Too many staff meetings took up too much time.

Accounting couldn't get costs to us when we needed them.

The schedule was unrealistic.

It's a sales issue.

The client's wife didn't like it.

The team leader quit at the last minute.

Work Excuses

Management insisted on hiring consultants.

The project team was full of incompetents.

I wasn't given enough authority.

The team leader turned out to be obsessed with micro-managing.

The designer department gave the client too many options.

Too many software issues.

The cost overruns were all the management's doing.

Getting the municipal permits took forever.

The Arts: Writers and Musicians

Piano:

My fingers are too short to reach that distance.

I just got my piano tuned and I want to keep it that way.

After a while, all the white keys look the same.

I'm used to playing baby grands—I never played a spinet.

Those black keys keep getting in my way.

Guitar:

My fingers are too fat to make that chord.

Clapton plays it that way, and he's God.

No rock song can be too loud.

Work Excuses

I'm missing several fingers. [So was Django Reinhardt. —Ed.]

I'm waiting to grow calluses.

I though a power chord would fit in there.

I'm developing my own style.

The battery in the tuner died.

I just wanna rock!

Wind Instruments:

There's water in the tone holes.

I play a bugle—these trumpet values are confusing.

The reed is too thick/thin.

The dog ate my reeds.

Excuses for All Occasions

The valve stuck.

The stand is too high.

String Instruments:

New strings.

The rosin is too sticky.

The peg slipped.

Vibrato, rubato—same difference.

My strap broke.

The banjo head needs tightening.

Drums:

I brought the wrong sticks.

Can't you hear that I'm playing the off-beat.

Work Excuses

If the guitars and bass didn't play so loud, they could hear me.

The dog chewed on the stick.

My hand hurts.

Someone was fooling with the tympani's tuning knobs.

Someone was messing with the high hat.

Nobody's listening to my beat.

Choir and Chorus:

I'm really a second soprano.

The basses came in late.

I can't hear the soloist.

I can't see the director.

Excuses for All Occasions

The tenors are throwing me off.

The accompaniment is throwing me off.

The alto line went above ours.

I like the other arrangement better.

I've always sung that note with a fermata.

I think there's a typo in the music.

The sopranos are singing too loud.

Orchestra:

CONDUCTOR: You came in two bars too late.
PLAYER: The guy who usually sits next to me does the counting for me, but he isn't here.
PLAYER: I only know the third trumpet part here not the first trumpet part.

Work Excuses

CONDUCTOR: But all three trumpets are in unison here.

CONDUCTOR: Can't you read music?
PERCUSSIONIST: Not so it hurts my playing.

CONDUCTOR: That note should have been a D.
VIOLINIST: My fingers insisted it was a C#.

Writers Who Are Late Delivering Their Manuscripts:

My computer crashed and ate my manuscript.

It must have gotten lost in the mail.

I had a scheduling conflict.

My agent said she's help me with the editing, but she's out of town for the rest of the year.

Excuses for All Occasions

Just as I was about to finish the article, I thought of a better way to write it, but that way requires much more research.

There was an illness in the family.

My editor moved to another publisher, and I'd like to follow him there.

My day job is taking up too much time.

Someone told me that your magazine folded.

The economy is so bad I have to hold down three jobs.

Another publisher came out with a book on the same subject, and it's better than mine would be.

My home office was flooded, and the manuscript washed away.

My agent said he'd get a contract extension, but then he disappeared.

4.

"School days, school days, dear old 'the dog ate my homework' days . . . ." The majority of excuses in these categories show an imagination that would get an A-plus in any Creative Writing class. The others get a D for "Desperation."

Absences and Tardiness

Please excuse me for the rest of the day as the cafeteria food made me delirious.

I was late for class because the bell rang before I got here.

I won't be in class because my dog chipped my tooth.

I was late for school five days in a row: the first four days were because of flat tires, and then all the clocks in the house stopped at once, and I was unable to tell the time.

School Excuses

I had a good excuse for not attending the class, but I forgot—so please excuse me for forgetting my excuse for not attending the class.

I could not make it to school today because my sister went into labor as she was driving me to school. Enclosed is a picture of my new baby niece.

I don't have a written excuse for being late, but here's the phone number of the man whose mailbox I hit.

I was late to school because when I woke up this morning, my medulla oblongata just felt really funny.

I could not come to class because I live on the second floor, and early in the morning the landlord came along and removed the steps to my apartment.

[The teacher's comment] She might have been fine if she'd stopped there, but she went on with her daring and heroic escape facilitated by a downspout. The downspout had climbing roses growing up it, which made the ensuing slide all the more perilous . . . if the young woman had put half the thought into her papers as she did this story, she would have graduated with honors.

School Excuses

Notes from Parents

My son is under a doctor's care and should not take P.E. today. Please execute him.

Please excuse Lisa for being absent. She was sick and I had her shot.

Dear Mrs. Teacher: Please excuse Harry for not being at school for two weeks because he had all his hair cut off his head.

Dear School: Please excuse John being absent on Jan. 28, 29, 30, 31, 32, and also 33.

Please excuse Gloria from Jim today. She is administrating.

Please excuse Robert from gym class for a few days. Yesterday he fell out of a tree and misplaced his hip.

Excuses for All Occasions

Jimmy has been absent because he had two teeth taken out of his face.

Carlos was absent yesterday because he was playing football. He was hurt in the growing part.

Please excuse my daughter from school. We told her two days ago that her mother is her grandma, her sister is her mother, and daddy is still daddy, and she hasn't come out of the bedroom since.

Please excuse Ricky from school yesterday. He had spilled gasoline on his stomach and was afraid he would explode.

Megan could not come to school today because she has been bothered by very close veins.

Please excuse Ray Friday from school. He has very loose vowels.

School Excuses

Please excuse Tommy for being absent yesterday. He had diarrhea and his boots leak.

Elizabeth was absent yesterday because she missed the bust.

Please excuse Jimmy for being. It was his father's fault.

I kept Maggie home because she had to go Christmas shopping since I don't know what size she wears.

Please excuse Jennifer for missing school yesterday. We forgot to get the Sunday paper off the porch, and when we found it Monday, we thought it was Sunday.

Sally won't be in school a week from Friday. We have to attend her funeral.

Excuses for All Occasions

My daughter was absent yesterday because she was tired. She spent a weekend with the Marines.

Please excuse Jason for being absent yesterday. He had a cold and could not breed well.

Please excuse Mary for being absent yesterday. She was in bed with gramps.

Gloria was absent yesterday as she was having a hangover.

Please excuse Josie who has been sick and under the doctor.

Maryanne was absent December 11–16, because she had a fever, sore throat, headache, and upset stomach. Her sister was also sick, had a fever, and a sore throat. Her brother had a low grade fever, and a ached all over. I wasn't the best either and had a sore throat and fever. There must be something going around—her father even got hot last night.

School Excuses

Please excuse Bob from school from Sep. 1–Nov. 1. He had to attend a religious sacrificial giving ceremony on Indian grounds.

Please excuse my daughter for being late. Her broom won't start so I had to send it back to Salem for repairs.

Please excuse my son from being absent as it was Senior Skip Day.

Please excuse Eric from school on May 5th thru May 19th. He was waiting in line for the new *Star Wars* film. You will be happy to know he got tickets for next September, when he will be missing another week of school while he waits for the perfect seat.

Please excuse Marie from school yesterday. It was Take Your Daughter To Work day. I don't have a job, so I made her stay home and do housework.

Excuses for All Occasions

Please excuse my daughter from school yesterday and P.E. forever. She had a very bad asthma attack running in P.E. because the coach made her run too much. Please excuse her from P.E. even though the doctor says she needs it.

Please excuse Henry for being late for school. He was stuck in the bathroom without any toilet paper.

Dear Teacher: Please excuse my son from being absent from school Friday. Some stupid school superintendent wouldn't close the schools due to the ice storm and even though we live across the street from the school, I wasn't about to send him out and have him break his neck falling on a huge sheet of ice on the ground. I wasn't about to go out with him to help him to school and fall and break my neck either.

Please excuse my son from school yesterday because he didn't feel like going.

School Excuses

I was late because I was stuck behind a slow-driving tractor-trailer. Here's a note from the tractor-trailer driver saying he was driving slowly.

Johnny was late today because of a shallow gene pool.

My daughter was not at school all last week because her father (my ex-husband) picked her up for a visit and did not return her for six days. If you want to know where she was, you'll have to ask him, as I still don't know.

A parent in December 1999 sent a note saying that her son would miss a week of school due to the family attending a millennium-survival workshop "just in case."

Excuses for All Occasions

Classroom Excuses: Students to Teachers regarding Homework and Tests

My dog ate my homework.

[French class] *Mon chien a mangé mes devoirs.*

[Spanish class] *Mi perro comió mi tarea.*

My dad got a new paper shredder for his home office, and while we were testing it out, it ate my homework.

My snake died, and I just wasn't in the mood for thinking.

My father used my homework to start a fire.

I didn't want to do my homework and add to your already staggering workload.

What? Didn't you feel the earthquake?

70

School Excuses

Although I have known the subject of my final project for three months now, I could not turn it in on time because I am not able to type so fast.

I couldn't turn my homework in because my little brother stole it, filled it in and turned it in to his teacher to prove how smart he was.

I couldn't do my homework because it got all dark outside.

I bumped into Lady Gaga last night, and she thought my essay would make a really good song, so she took it and will be returning it soon.

Handing in homework on Friday the 13th is considered to bring really bad luck to both student and teacher.

I was doing my homework when my mother suddenly started a grease fire on the stove top, and I had to smother her with my homework so that she wouldn't die.

My attorney advised me to respond "no comment" regarding the whereabouts of my alleged homework at this time.

Yesterday's service project was to fill sandbags to help protect houses from mudslides. We finished in the late afternoon, but I had to stay to be interviewed by six different television crews. Do you know how long it takes to do six interviews? I was so tired, I had to sleep in. I taped the interviews for you, and I'd appreciate it if you would accept them in place of my homework.

Am I supposed to bring homework to school? I thought it stayed at home.

I don't have my homework because I put it down on the kitchen counter, and my mother never cleans the kitchen.

School Excuses

SpellCheck says you can spell that word that way, too.

I did my homework and then my dad wanted to check it. While he was checking it, his boss phoned saying that he had to pack because he was going out of town. Well, he was in such a hurry, he packed my homework in his suitcase. He won't be back for another three weeks, so I need an extension.

[Math class] I must have forgotten to carry the number into the next column.

There's an Occupy Wall Street [or wherever else] rally tonight, so I need an extension on my homework.

My locker is jammed, and I can't get my homework out of it.

Then you don't understand the "new math."

Excuses for All Occasions

You never said that would be on the test.

But who uses this stuff in the real world?

[Gym class] I can't participate because I left my gym clothes at home.

I use only recycled paper, and the store was out of it.

Blame it on school spirit—how could I be expected to miss last night's pep rally?

How can I be expected to learn so many details?

I didn't do my homework because of my eyes. I couldn't see any reason to do it.

Doesn't refuting the essay question count for anything?

School Excuses

I couldn't do the assignment because I have the world's worst case of Seasonal Affective Disorder.

[English literature] You'll have to admit that one sonnet looks pretty much like another.

I did the homework in my head. You never said it had to be written down.

But you've been asking another question on the midterm every other year.

[French class] My roommate spent a weekend in Paris and she said the French never use that expression.

[Geology] All those rocks look pretty much alike.

A segment on the nightly news said that the brain works better when it has sufficient rest.

Excuses for All Occasions

Do you value my health above a homework assignment?

It's not plagiarism, it's "eclectic research."

[Art History] All those Italian Renaissance artist names sound pretty much alike.

Doesn't "printer error" mean just that?—the printer made the mistake, I didn't.

[Science class] It's called an experiment—how else could I prove that's how you make gunpowder?

Would you take that tone of voice with Stephen Hawkin or Albert Einstein? I think not.

Wikipedia has that error in fact, too? What a coincidence!

My desktop crashed and—wouldn't you know it?—the external hard drive did, too.

School Excuses

[Theater Arts] Sorry, but I couldn't find my motivation.

Objective tests never let you express yourself.

Essay tests are too vague. You don't know what's expected.

Weekly tests require too much studying and not enough time for learning.

Doesn't classroom participation count for anything?

Doesn't attitude count for anything?

Without tests, how can the teacher judge what I've learned?

But we never even discussed that in class.

Excuses for All Occasions

Biologists at Indiana State University say that birds can sleep with both eyes closed and their whole brain asleep, or they can rest half their brain by keeping one eye shut. "Birds have overcome the problem of sleeping in risky situations by developing the ability to sleep with one eye open and one hemisphere of the brain awake," the scientists report in the journal *Nature*. Well, in an attempt to see whether other species can do that too, I've been experimenting, and apparently I am able to allow half my brain to fall asleep. The problem is, I haven't been able to wake it at times, and so I took that exam with only half my brain, and therefore—in the interest of science—I deserve to take the exam over.

I started out for the library, but I decided to have a quick beer first. By the way, that was your wife I saw you with in that bar last night, wasn't it? If it was, she sure looks young for her age.

School Excuses

STUDENT: Will you get mad at me for something I didn't do?

TEACHER: No.

STUDENT: Promise?

TEACHER: Yes.

STUDENT: Well then, I didn't do my homework.

A teacher who announced the date for the class's final exam added that there would be no excuses for not showing up barring a dire medical condition or an immediate family member's death.

The class clown asked, "What about extreme sexual exhaustion?"

After the laughter had subsided, the teacher glared at the boy and said, "That's not an acceptable excuse—you can use your other hand to write."

"Don't make excuses, make something incredible happen in your life right now."

—*Greg Hickman*

5.

Some enchanted evening you look across a crowded room and your eyes catch an object of desire. Or standing next to you at a bar or a Starbucks is someone you're attracted to, and he or she has the same reaction. You two talk, date, fall in love, and stay in love for ever and ever.

Yeah, sure—that's the way it happens, right? Maybe in the movies or a romance novel, but in real life the path to love can be strewn with semi-truths, outright lies, and rejections.

Among the myriad examples of the last are several classics, beginning with the "it's over before it begins" category that includes rebuffing pick-up lines and turning down a second date. You don't want to dump all over the person, you just want to dump him or her, so you want ways to let the person down easy while getting yourself off the hook. And if you come up with an excuse that makes you sound a little flakey to the point that the person would lose interest in you, then so much the better.

Romance (or the Lack Thereof)

You're not my type.

You remind me of an old boyfriend/girlfriend/ex-spouse, and I know you'd break my heart, too.

I know I'm shallow, and I know I place too high a value on physical appeal, but . . .

You're voting for WHO?!

I've got to wash my hair tomorrow night.

I'm gay.

I don't buy into that what's-your-sign astrology crap.

How could you not like that movie? I couldn't like anyone who doesn't like Brad Pitt [or Angela Jolie or Jackie Chan or the Smurfs].

What if we were twins separated at birth?

I know just the guy/gal for you . . . let me fix you up.

You're an Aries and I'm a Pisces—we'd never work out.

I'm a very religious person, and I can see that you're not.

I find that sort of politically incorrect remark inexcusable in the extreme.

You're the type of man/woman I always get into trouble with.

How can you not like dogs/cats/parakeets/tropical fish/snakes?

It's not you . . . it's me.

You're really a lovely person, and I know you'll find someone, but that isn't me.

Personal Life Excuses

Now, let's say you have that second date and then a third and a fourth, and before you know it you're in love or "in like" or however you choose to character-ize the relationship. But—there are always "buts"—you wake up one day and decide that the person isn't really for you and you want out. How do you handle the situation?

If an explanation (included but not limited to the truth) would be too hurtful, you'll need an excuse. Some of the above ones are "classics" for this circum-stance, too: the "lovely person, but," and "it's not you, it's me," for example. But there are many others:

An old boyfriend/girlfriend came back into my life.

We rushed into this too fast, and I'm scared.

My landlord doesn't like you, and I don't want to be evicted.

I can tell that your friends don't like me.

Excuses for All Occasions

You're too kinky for my taste.

I'm getting married this weekend, so I won't be able to see you again.

You don't understand the difference between "love" and "in love."

You obviously have some hang-ups that you have to work out.

You're way too overprotective.

You're always trying to psychoanalyze me—you're not my shrink!

It turns out that I don't like you in that way.

There's this guy/gal at work I'm really attracted to . . . .

I can't stand your politics.

Personal Life Excuses

I need my space.

You snore.

I don't want you to become too attached.

Trust me, you'll be better off.

You're too messy, and you never clean up after yourself. I'm not your maid.

We just don't like the same things.

Don't ask about the sex—I don't want to hurt your feelings.

You're too manipulative.

Don't think I didn't see you flirting with my roommate.

You deserve better.

Your Cheating Heart

In no other area of human endeavor does Sir Walter Scott's observation that "Oh! what a tangled web we weave/when first we practice to deceive" apply more than affairs of the heart.

Actually, it's not always the heart. When a 19th-century actress asked an attentive French politician whether he was after her heart, he replied, "Mademoiselle, I am not aiming that high." And speaking of politicians and other celebrities, it seems that they occupy more than their fair share of the Excuses Hall of Fame/Shame. Cases in point:

"Because I could."

> —*President Bill Clinton's justification for his Oval Office dalliances with Monica Lewinsky.*

"It depends upon what the meaning of the word 'is' is. If the—if he—if 'is' means is and never

Personal Life Excuses

has been, that is not—that is one thing. If it means there is none, that was a completely true statement."

—President Clinton, contending that there was no ongoing relationship with Ms. Lewinsky at the time he was asked the question at a grand jury deposition.

"Yes, he has weaknesses. Yes, he needs to be more disciplined, but it is remarkable given his background that he turned out to be the kind of person he is, capable of such leadership. [He is] a hard dog to keep on the porch."

—Hilary Clinton, explaining her husband's infidelity.

"I've had my lapses with other women, sure— welcome to the music business."

—rock musician Jon Bon Jovi, on his many marital infidelities.

Excuses for All Occasions

"[I was] partially driven by how passionately I felt about this country . . . I worked far too hard and things happened in my life that were not appropriate."

—former Speaker of the House Newt Gingrich, on his two marriage-ending infidelities.

"The heart wants what it wants."

—film actor/writer/director Woody Allen, explaining why he had an affair with the adopted daughter of actress Mia Farrow, with whom he had a relationship.

"Nude massage."

—ex-Senator and Governor Charles "Chuck" Robb (and husband of President Lyndon Johnson's daughter, Lynda) on why he was found in a hotel room with a former Miss Virginia.

Personal Life Excuses

"There's nothing so similar to one poodle dog as another poodle dog, and that goes for women, too."

—artist Pablo Picasso on his many marital infidelities.

"In the course of several campaigns, I started to believe that I was special and became increasingly narcissistic."

—former Senator John Edwards, justifying his affair with a former campaign worker.

And from one head(ache) of state to another: President John Kennedy justified his affairs to British Prime Minister Harold Macmillan with, "I wonder how it is with you, Harold? If I don't have a woman for three days, I get terrible headaches."

Excuses for All Occasions

We know how well the above excuses worked, but you're free to try them if and when you're caught. If not, any of these "becauses" may work better:

Because you don't take very good care of yourself.

Because you take me for granted.

Because all I hear from you is nag, nag, nag.

Because we lead such different lives now.

Because I wanted to shake up our relationship and make it grow stronger.

Because we've drifted apart.

Because I was tempted.

Because I'm not getting any younger, and I was feeling my age.

Personal Life Excuses

Because I don't love you anymore.

If the "because"s don't fit, there are others, such as:

It was just a fling.

Dr. Phil calls it an addiction.

These things don't mean anything.

I'll never see that person again.

It wasn't planned—I just don't know what came over me.

He/she sounded so unhappy that I wanted to comfort him/her.

My doctor said it was part of my midlife crisis.

When you spend that much time at the office with someone, something's bound to happen.

It's a guy thing . . . something like the onset of male menopause.

Women need romance, and he gave it to me.

I'm just not as strong-willed as I thought I was.

It doesn't mean I don't love you.

Okay, so I owe you one.

I was going to tell you about it, but you found out first.

Are you going to believe me or your lying eyes?

Not Getting Married

I haven't found the right person yet.

Sooner or later you start taking the other person for granted.

My career comes first. I'll marry if and when I achieve job satisfaction.

I'm too young.

I like being able to do what I want whenever I want to do it.

All my married friends seem so unhappy.

Commitment scares me.

Wearing white makes me look fat.

I was head-over-heels in love with my high school sweetheart who dumped me, and I'm dreaming of the day she gets divorced and comes crawling back to me.

Excuses for All Occasions

My boyfriend/girlfriend refuses to sign a pre-nup.

I'm way too old.

Finding the right person is too damned hard.

Marriage is a dying institution.

Who'd want his/her parents for in-laws?

I was married before—once burnt, twice shy.

I've been living alone for a long time, and I'm far too set in my ways.

We don't want children, so why bother getting married?

Not getting married is the surest way of making sure you'll never get divorced.

According to my accountant, I'd increase my tax liability.

Why buy the cow if you can milk it through the fence?

Not Having Children

I will not be adding to an already overpopulated planet.

I can decorate my house anyway I want to, including with breakable and hazardous-to-children items.

Who needs a phone call in the middle of the night from the hospital or the police because of something my child did?

I'll never be compared to someone else's parent or another family's lifestyle.

Nobody will try to ride the dog, pull the cat's tail, or drop toys into the tropical fish tank.

The house will be quiet . . . all the time.

Excuses for All Occasions

If my marriage is coming apart, my spouse and I won't feel as though we have to stay married "because of the kid(s)."

I won't have to watch my language.

I won't have to wipe noses or change diapers or clean up after my child throws up.

I can go to bed whenever I like and then get a good night's sleep.

I'll save hundreds of thousands of dollars on college educations.

I can travel anywhere and at all times of year.

The house will be neater and cleaner.

I can live in a smaller and therefore less expensive home.

Personal Life Excuses

Weekends and vacations can be spent however I want to spend them.

I can watch television programs and movies that I want to see.

Mealtimes will always be civilized, and they can be whenever I feel like eating.

I can be alone or with people with whom I choose to be whenever and wherever I choose.

Not Exercising

My dog ate my running shoe.

I have to get in better shape before I can join a gym.

Wearing a leotard makes me look like a bratwurst.

I used to take a taxi to the gym, but it became too costly.

Riding a bike in the city is too dangerous.

I'll never look like Angela Jolie/Jane Fonda/Johnny Depp/Harrison Ford, so why bother?

I'm too tired to exercise.

My running shoe's lace broke.

Personal Life Excuses

The mirrors at the health club make me look fat.

Sweating makes my makeup run and then my skin breaks out.

I don't have time.

Treadmills and stationary bicycles are boring.

Health club memberships are expensive.

"Whenever I get the urge to exercise, I lie down until the feeling passes away."

—Robert M. Hutchins

"I have never taken any exercise, except for sleeping and resting, and I never intend to take any. Exercise is loathsome."

—Mark Twain

"I get my exercise acting as a pallbearer to my friends who exercise."

—Chauncey Depew

"I do not participate in any sport with ambulances at the bottom of a hill."

—Erma Bombeck on skiing.

Not Losing Weight

I wasn't getting enough to eat on one diet so I had to go on three.

It's winter, and I need the extra insulation to keep me warm.

My mother becomes very upset if I don't eat everything she serves me, and she's a great cook.

I hate to see food spoil.

Everyone in my family has a weight problem, and you can't fight the genes.

Someone was on my favorite treadmill at the gym, so I had to skip that day.

Everyone gains weight with age.

They say people grow to resemble their pets, and I have a Saint Bernard and a bulldog.

Excuses for All Occasions

Medicine has great advances in liposuction.

Exercising makes me ravenously hungry.

Dieting makes me ravenously hungry.

Hey, you only live once.

My mother always made me clean my plate, and I can't break the habit.

How can you watch a football game without a beer or two and a bowl of chicken wings?

I watch what I eat, as it is.

I can't help it if I have a slow metabolism.

Losing weight takes too long.

If rice cakes have no calories, so must all other kinds of cake.

My trainer put on a few pounds, so I figured if he can, so can I.

Personal Life Excuses

Who wants to think about not eating all day?

Being aware of everything I eat is stressful, and stress makes me put on weight.

I'll just gain back the weight.

If I don't eat it, someone else will.

I can't afford to have my clothes taken in or buy a new wardrobe.

I don't want to insult my coworkers by not eating their birthday cakes.

I was just kidding about going on a diet.

"I refuse to spend my life worrying about what I eat. There is no pleasure worth foregoing just for an extra three years in the geriatric ward."

—John Mortimer

To Have a Drink

It's 5 o'clock somewhere.

I can never remember whether you can start drinking when the sun is over the yardarm or below the yardarm. The sun's got to be either one, so let's have a drink.

Isn't today the birthday of the guy who invented beer cans? Well, if it isn't, it should be.

It's the anniversary of the Battle of Saratoga/ Battle of Bull Run/Battle of San Jacinto/Charge Up San Juan Hill. Let's have a drink to the memory of our gallant troops.

Churchill and Roosevelt drank. Hitler didn't. I don't want to be mistaken for a Nazi.

That guy in Human Resources told me his sister-in-law just had twins. Let's drink to the dear little babies' health.

Personal Life Excuses

Alcohol in moderation raises high-density lipoprotein or HDL, known as good cholesterol.

We'll always have Paris—here's looking at you, kid.

Let's drink to [insert name of favorite team] having a better year next year.

A Harvard study reported that moderate beer consumption contributed to increased mental capacity in older women.

If you don't drink that Scotch, then someone else will.

The brewing industry alone employs close to two million people, and that's a lot of mouths to feed.

I just got a raise—let me buy you a drink.

I just got fired—buy me a drink.

I'm thirsty.

• • •

Excuses for All Occasions

And some literary excuses (all right, call them "reasons" if you must):

"[Wine] sloweth age, it strengtheneth youth, it helpeth digestion, it abandoneth melancholie, it relisheth the heart, it lighteneth the mind, it quickenth the spirits, it keepeth and preserveth the head from whirling, the eyes from dazzling, the tongue from lisping, the mouth from snaffling, the teeth from chattering and the throat from rattling; it keepeth the stomach from wambling, the heart from swelling, the hands from shivering, the sinews from shrinking, the veins from crumbling, the bones from aching, and the marrow from soaking."

—16th-Century anonymous writer

"Port is not for the very young, the vain and the active. It is the comfort of age and the companion of the scholar and the philosopher."

—Evelyn Waugh

Personal Life Excuses

"Show me a total abstainer that ever lived that long."

—*Will Rogers*

"In victory, you deserve champagne; in defeat, you need it."

—*Napoleon*

"An intelligent man is sometimes forced to be drunk to spend time with his fools."

—*Ernest Hemingway*

"Wine makes daily living easier, less hurried, with fewer tensions and more tolerance."

—*Benjamin Franklin*

Excuses for All Occasions

"If penicillin can cure those that are ill, Spanish sherry can bring the dead back to life."

— Sir Alexander Fleming

"If all be true that I do think, there are five reasons we should drink. Good friends, good times, or being dry, or lest we should be by and by, or any other reason why."

—anonymous

"Sometimes when I reflect on all the beer I drink, I feel ashamed. Then I look into the glass and think about the workers in the brewery and all of their hopes and dreams. If I didn't drink this beer, they might be out of work and their dreams would be shattered. I think, 'It is better to drink this beer and let their dreams come true than be selfish and worry about my liver.'"

—attributed to Babe Ruth

Personal Life Excuses

"Well ya see, Norm, it's like this. A herd of buffalo can only move as fast as the slowest buffalo. And when the herd is hunted, it is the slowest and weakest ones at the back that are killed first. This natural selection is good for the herd as a whole, because the general speed and health of the whole group keeps improving by the regular killing of the weakest members. In much the same way, the human brain can only operate as fast as the slowest brain cells. Excessive intake of alcohol, as we know, kills brain cells. But naturally, it attacks the slowest and weakest brain cells first. In this way, regular consumption of beer eliminates the weaker brain cells, making the brain a faster and more efficient machine! That's why you always feel smarter after a few beers."

—Cliff Clavin on the TV show Cheers.

"As soon as I step on the court I just try to play tennis and don't find excuses. You know, I just lost because I lost, not because my arm was sore."

—*Goran Ivanisevic*

6.

S port involves competition. There are winners and losers. Losers don't like losing, so they find excuses. It's as simple as that.

Sports Classics

"I managed good, but boy, they played bad."

—*baseball player-turned-manager Rocky Bridges*

"I lost it in the sun."

—*baseball player Billy Loes, explaining why he made an error fielding a ground ball.*

"But I never bet on them to lose."

—*baseball player Pete Rose on wagering on games in which his team was involved.*

Sports and Games Excuses

"We lost because we didn't win."

—*soccer player Cristiano Ronaldo*

"This is my career. I got children to raise and he keeps butting me. I got to retaliate."

—*boxer Mike Tyson, on why he bit opponent Evander Holyfield's ear during a fight.*

"I'm not saying my golf game went bad, but if I grew tomatoes, they'd come up sliced."

—*golfer Lee Trevino*

"I was getting carried away playing Tekken II and Tomb Raider for hours on end."

—*British soccer goalkeeper David James, on why his loss of concentration allowed the opposing team to score.*

Excuses for All Occasions

"I never lost a game in my life, I just ran out of time."

—football quarterback Bobby Layne

"I slept funny and couldn't blink."

—baseball player Jose Cardinal, on why he missed the Chicago Cubs' opening game of the 1974 season.

"We all agreed we would take some sticks and go and hunt them."

—Ukranian soccer player who, together with his teammates, blamed their World Cup loss to Spain because croaking frogs outside their hotel windows kept the team awake all night before the game.

Sports and Games Excuses

"I wasn't choking P.J. I mean, P.J., he could breathe. It's not like he was losing air or anything like that. I mean, it wasn't a choke. I wasn't trying to kill P.J."

Then when asked about the scratches around the coach's neck: "If you're choking someone, you don't get scratches, you get welts totally around your neck."

—basketball player Latrell Sprewell, on grabbing coach P.J. Carlesimo around the neck.

"My lace is broken!"

—figure skater Tonya Harding, after missing a triple jump during the 1994 Winter Olympics.

Excuses for All Occasions

"I'm not going to make any excuses. I just went out and stunk it up tonight."

—baseball player David Wells

"The team drew the match because the balls were too bouncy."

—English soccer manager Kenny Dalglish

"Our goalkeeper let in an easy equalizer as he was on his mobile phone with his girlfriend. He could not do it on the side of the field as his wife was there."

—unnamed British soccer team manager

Sports and Games Excuses

"It's where I keep my jewelry."

—football player Michael Vick, after an airport security scanner detected a hidden compartment in his water bottle containing evidence of marijuana residue.

English soccer goalkeeper Chris Mooney once contended that a simple shot went through his legs because a bald teammate's head created such a shine that it blinded his vision.

"I'm 23 years old, and despite the successes I've had in the pool, I acted in a youthful and inappropriate way, not in a manner people have come to expect from me."

—world champion swimmer Michael Phelps, after have been caught smoking marijuana.

Excuses for All Occasions

"I don't even know the total number for sure. I had serious blackouts. There were times when I would get up in the morning and nobody ever wanted to tell me what I lost. I didn't know whether I lost $50,000 or $500,000."

—Philadelphia Eagles owner Leonard Tose, excusing his highrolling gambling habit.

"It's my evil twin's fault."

—bicycle racer Tyler Hamilton, on hearing that antidoping testing indicated someone else's red blood cells were mixed with his. He blamed it on a twin who was reabsorbed while in the womb.

"I know I am surprised and I'm sure my fans are surprised given the clean lifestyle I live. I don't know how this could have happened."

—baseball player David "Big Papi" Ortiz, on using steroids.

Sports and Games Excuses

"They must have 'misremembered' that I was using HGH when I really wasn't."

—*baseball player Roger Clemens, on being accused of using growth hormones.*

"When he said it was flaxseed oil, I just said, 'Whatever.'"

—*baseball player Barry Bonds, after testing positive for steroids, contending he had no idea how his trainer was treating him.*

Football linebacker Brian Cushing, having tested positive for growth hormone HCG, claimed it was because he has a medical condition resulting from "overtrained athlete syndrome."

Other Excuses for Failing Drug Tests:

Baseball player Rafael Palmeiro claimed steroids were in vitamins that a teammate gave him.

Spanish discus thrower David Martinez blamed infected pigmeat.

Czech tennis player Petr Korda blamed eating too much veal.

British shotputter Paul Edwards attributed testing positive to having drunk shampoo.

Chinese track coach Ma Junren attributed three of his record-setting runners testing positive on a supplement that contained dried caterpillars and turtle blood.

Sports and Games Excuses

German runner Dieter Baumann attributed a failed steroid test to someone injecting his toothpaste with the drug.

High jumper Javier Sotomayor blamed a positive cocaine test on the CIA or an anti-Cuban mafia spiking his food, an explanation with which Premier Fidel Castro agreed.

Uzbekistan track coach Sergei Voynov said he used growth hormone to treat baldness.

British bobsledder Lenny Paul claimed he had eaten spoiled spaghetti Bolognese.

And the gold medal for the all-time sports excuse:

"Musumba Bwayla is a stupid man and a hopeless player. He has a huge nose and is crosseyed. Girls hate him. He beat me because my jockstrap was too tight and because when he serves he farts, and that made me lose my concentration, for which I am famous throughout Zambia."

—Zambian tennis player Lighton Ndefwayl, on why he lost a match to rival Musumba Bwayla.

Sports

Now, for the rest of us, and feel free to borrow from other sports . . .

Baseball and Softball:

The grounder took a funny hop.

I couldn't find my good glove . . . . Ever try playing first with an outfielder's mitt?

She ran way out of the base path.

Someone broke my lucky bat.

I haven't played third base in years.

I tripped over a rock in the outfield.

I'm used to slow-pitch softball.

I did so tag him.

I thought there were two outs.

Excuses for All Occasions

Maybe if the cutoff man was there in time . . .

The other team is much younger than we are.

Artificial turf is too slippery after it rains.

These spikes don't grab on this surface.

I didn't take one for the team I couldn't get out of the way in time.

I twisted my ankle sliding into second.

The ump's strike zone is too small.

They're corking their bats!

I'm not used to wooden bats.

I could hit that many home runs too if I were on steroids.

The right field fence is too close—no wonder everybody hit my pitching.

It was a pitchers' ballpark.

Sports and Games Excuses

It was a batters' ballpark

I lost it in the sun.

Football:

I did so touch him with both hands.

Illegal block!

The other team's quarterback was a ringer. I'm sure I saw his photo in *Sports Illustrated*.

That pass was too wobbly—can't anyone throw a decent spiral?

She tripped me.

The coach took me out too soon.

My contact lens slipped.

The ball is under-inflated.

That was a late whistle.

Excuses for All Occasions

The ball is too wet—my fingers slipped off the laces.

I didn't hear the snap.

I twisted my ankle.

I was clipped!

How do you expect me to get past that guy? He's a monster!

Can't anyone block for me?

That wasn't my man to defend.

I didn't know the play.

The other team knew the play.

The ball isn't the size I'm used to throwing.

I forgot my gloves.

The snow was blowing right in my eyes.

Sports and Games Excuses

He didn't hold the ball right for my field goal try.

They were icing the kicker.

My teammates dropped the easiest, wide-open passes.

The backup QB is no good.

The halftime show was so bad, it made the Lions lose the Thanksgiving Day game.

I lost it in the sun.

Basketball:

I was fouled.

The other team cheats.

I haven't played in a week.

My sneakers hurt.

Hey, I gave it my best shot.

Excuses for All Occasions

The ball is under-inflated.

The hoop is too wobbly.

The ref gives quick whistles.

Hey ref, that's hacking where I come from.

The coach left me in too long.

The lighting in this gym is bad.

That guy under the board outweighs me by 50 pounds.

The court slopes.

I twisted my ankle two plays ago.

My teammates stink.

I wasn't traveling—she tripped me!

I didn't have time to warm up.

I'm getting too old for this game.

Sports and Games Excuses

I'm saving myself for the playoffs.

This league has too many games.

I had to miss practice all last week.

Illegal defense!

I'm beat—I played last night, too.

I was fouled again.

I lost it in the sun/in the lights.

Golf:

I can't grip the club the way I used to—darn this wedding ring.

Somebody stole my ball.

My knee hurts.

The guys I usually play with are generous with mulligans.

Excuses for All Occasions

The drive must have hit something when it landed.

The putting green was faster than this one.

Damn goose poop all over my shoe.

There was a bug on my ball.

This driver needs a new grip.

The course where I play has pine trees—these maples are distracting me.

That lie was in between clubs.

That gust of wind knocked my approach shot off line.

My caddie gave me the wrong club.

The ball was in a divot.

I thought we were still playing winter rules.

My shoelace broke.

Sports and Games Excuses

The sun was in my eyes.

I don't remember that tree being there.

The putt rimmed out.

I was too hung over to concentrate.

That shot is easier to make on the video golf game.

Wait till I put on a few pounds—I'll drive 50 yards further.

I was standing too close to the ball (partner's retort: "Yeah, after you hit it.").

I don't know how I could have left my clubs at home—these rental ones stink.

That squirrel pushed my ball into the bunker.

That coffee you gave me couldn't have been decaf.

Wait till I take off a few pounds—my old swing will come back.

All the golf schools I liked were too expensive so I taught myself.

Bermuda grass is terrible—my clubs keep getting stuck.

Going back to the "interlocking" grip was a mistake.

You sneezed just when I putted.

I lost my lucky ball marker.

I play better with good players.

From three hundred yards out, it looks like the green sloped away. I should have laid up.

Golf is about etiquette, not playing well.

Sports and Games Excuses

Excuses to Play Golf:

The dealer gave me a free round for test-driving that car.

I need more practice understanding all the rules of the game.

It'll be a good career move—all the executives from my company play this course.

All the pin placements are forward today.

Church was cancelled because of the bad weather.

Frustration is a rush. I can only get that on a golf course.

Golf is the only place I can take my girlfriend where she can't talk constantly.

Golf teaches me patience, and I need a lesson.

The more I play, the better I get.

I almost broke 90 last time out—maybe I will today.

I always play well when it rains.

I'm almost 50; I need to practice for the senior circuit.

Ice Hockey:

I broke my favorite stick.

I tripped over my lace.

I was high-sticked.

The puck took a bad hop.

The ice is too bumpy.

I was hooked from behind.

I lost my edge.

Sports and Games Excuses

I'm used to playing on ponds, not in these indoor rinks.

My helmet slipped over my eyes.

It was three on one.

The cage is too small.

The ice is too soft.

I think I chipped a tooth.

Volleyball:

Those guys are giants!

The referee called too loose.

My shorts kept slipping when I jumped.

There's not enough room around the court.

The ball was too hard/too soft.

Excuses for All Occasions

The reflection off the sand made the soles of my feet sunburned.

The floor was too slippery.

The sand was too hot.

The sun was in my eyes when I served.

The set was too far off the net.

He touched the net!

That blonde in the front row distracted me.

The other team served too tough.

The other team didn't make any mistakes.

Tennis:

I wasn't ready for that serve.

The sun got into my eyes.

It's too hot.

Sports and Games Excuses

I'm too short to play a big game. I'm better in a serve-and-volley situation.

My racquet grip is loose.

My sneaker lace came untied.

This court needs a windscreen.

I still think that shot hit the line.

I never played on grass before.

Balls from the other court distracted me.

My sock gave me a blister.

Sweat keeps getting in my eyes.

It's too dark to see the ball.

I ate too much breakfast/lunch/dinner.

My tennis elbow is acting up.

My partner let me down.

Excuses for All Occasions

My racquet needed new strings.

The tournament seeding makes no sense.

My opponent called all my shots out.

My opponent got lucky.

That serve would have been good except for a damn gust of wind.

The balls are dead.

Fishing:

This lake is over-fished.

The net got tangled and I lost the fish.

The kids made too much noise and spooked the fish.

I lost my favorite top-water plug.

The fish are too well fed to go after bait.

Sports and Games Excuses

The brookies were taking #18 Adams Parachutes, and all I had were #16s.

It's too sunny.

I hurt my wrist, and I couldn't cast far enough.

Someone took my favorite spot.

It's too cloudy.

Someone gave me the wrong GPS coordinates.

My reel had the granddaddy of all backlashes

The wind's from the East [referring to the old saying: "Wind from the East, fish bite the least"].

It was the wrong phase of the moon.

The fish were hitting short.

The trolling motor broke.

Excuses for All Occasions

The guy in the next boat cast like a beginner and spooked all the fish.

The water's too warm/too cold.

The bass were hitting purple lures, and all I had was chartreuse.

The barometer was falling.

The hooks on my lucky spinnerbait were dull, and I couldn't find the sharpener.

The lodge owner said we should have been here last week.

The worms died.

I'll never get the hang of nymph fishing.

The line snapped—there must have been a twist or a kink.

I'm afraid of leeches.

The guide couldn't find any fish.

Sports and Games Excuses

The jigs were the wrong weight.

I retrieved the plug too fast.

I thought I had sunstroke.

There must be hatchery fish in here.

It's the fishing, not the catching, that matters.

Hunting:

There must have been something wrong with the sighting distances.

Whyever did I buy cut-rate ammo.

Too much wind today.

The wind blew a branch in front of my arrow.

This deer stand wobbles.

My cell phone rang just as I was ready to shoot.

The scope lens has a crack.

Excuses for All Occasions

It was too dark.

The duck blind leaked.

My dog needs more training.

The arrow must have been bent.

My kids must have been playing with my duck call.

All the deer have gone nocturnal.

There are too many hunters in the woods—nothing is moving.

There aren't enough hunters in the woods—nothing is moving.

Deer don't move in wind.

Deer don't move when it rains.

Deer don't move when it snows.

Deer don't move when it's too hot.

Deer don't move when it's too cold.

Damn, I had a full choke and I should have been using a modified.

I was up so early, I fell asleep in the blind.

The sun was in my eyes.

An Ohio deer hunter shot a deer and loaded it into his vehicle. In the process, the deer kicked the hunter's gun, which went off and wounded him in the leg. The hunter's excuse: he "thought the deer was deader than it was."

Horse Sports:

My saddle slipped.

I hear that judge hates [the name of the breed you're showing].

I left my lucky gloves at home.

Excuses for All Occasions

The cow quit too soon [for cutting horse competitors].

I slept through my early start time.

That was a cheap rail—it should have stayed up.

The course didn't walk that way at all.

My horse spooked at something and swapped leads.

My trainer said the line rode in a *forward* six strides.

That judge hates me.

My horse stumbled and threw me on the wrong diagonal right in front of the judge.

I'm used to riding with braided reins.

My horse jumped the bank at home just fine.

I'm really a header/heeler.

Sports and Games Excuses

The hazer let that calf get away.

I ride better in the morning.

Having my mother watch me makes me nervous.

I need a better pony.

My horse jumps better when the fences are higher.

I forgot the reining pattern.

I thought it was the other dressage test.

Nobody told me that's an illegal bit.

Horse Racing: Some Excuses for Betting on a Losing Horse

The jockey/driver wasn't trying.

The horse was boxed in down the back-stretch.

Excuses for All Occasions

I bet before the smart money bet on another horse . . . I should have waited.

I should have known that the horse that shipped in came to win.

My horse was going up in class.

My horse was going against older horses.

It had to be a boat race.

You just can't figure out first-time starters.

My horse jumped off his rider at the last fence.

My horse would have won with/without blinkers.

The pace was too slow—the winner stole the race.

Sports and Games Excuses

The outside post position killed him.

It rained at the last minute, and the horse is no mudder.

The race was switched from the turf to the dirt, and he's no dirt horse.

The trainer must have been waiting for better odds next time.

He bore out in the stretch.

The stewards should have/shouldn't have allowed the foul claim.

Games

Poker:

I'm just playing for fun.

It was late.

I was way down and got too desperate.

Lady Luck flipped her skirts in my face.

I was way up and got too cocky.

I had a feeling the hole card was a [fill in the blank].

I had just won a large pot so what was a few chips to me after that?

My game is roll-your-own, high-low-splits-the-pot, and nobody plays that anymore.

Stud [or draw, or another game] isn't my best game.

Nobody plays the percentages anymore.

Sports and Games Excuses

I was bored.

I couldn't get that last hand out of my mind.

I played badly in order to get all of my poor plays out of my system while I was waiting for a bigger game/tournament.

The room had too much smoke.

I was drinking.

Too many wild cards.

Too much chatter—I couldn't concentrate.

The cards were cold.

The guy on my left had bad breath.

The guy on my right kept peeking.

The stakes were too low for me to pay much attention.

I was dealt aces and eights—the "Dead Man's Hand"—and it scared me all night.

Bret Maverick once drew to an filled an inside straight. I thought I could, too.

I bet low holding a three, a four, a five, a six, and an eight. Who could have figured that the guy on my left held a two, a three, a four, a five, and a seven?

Craps:

The dice were cold.

Those were new dice/wornout dice.

The dice bounced off the table

One of the dice hit the rail/hit the stick.

One die landed on top of the other

The dice slipped out of my hand.

I heard someone say "seven."

It was just a bad table.

Sports and Games Excuses

Pool/Billiards:

The other guy got all the rails.

The table is too fast/too slow.

That kid left me nothing—nothing!

The felt hadn't been replaced since World War Two.

I got sharked.

The table slopes.

I left my good cue at home.

I usually play billiards, not pool.

I usually play pool, not billiards.

Chess:

My opponent shouldn't have played on in a lost position.

My perpetual check didn't last very long.

Excuses for All Occasions

I play better using my own set.

I played a knight sacrifice, but he took my queen instead.

That was just a lucky checkmate.

Where'd that rook come from?

Nobody heard me say *j'adoube*.

My strength is the end game, but I didn't get that far.

I became demoralized when I went a pawn down.

Who ever heard of taking a piece *en passant*?

The sacrifice just didn't work out the way I planned.

Nobody sees ten moves away.

The concept of white moving first is racist.

Chess glorifies war.

7.

Let's get serious for a moment. Traffic tickets are no joke, so here's some good advice in case you're stopped or pulled over:

Traffic Tickets

First and foremost, be polite and cooperative. Although a belligerent, sarcastic, or argumentative response may lower your blood pressure, such an attitude won't improve your position. The police regards traffic stops as potentially and unpredictably dangerous situations, so behave accordingly. Keep your hands in sight, preferably on the steering wheel. If you're stopped at night, turn on the car's interior lights. If you haven't gotten out your license, registration, and proof of insurance as soon as you stop, inform the officer that you must reach in your coat, pants, purse, or glove compartment.

Politeness, respect, and cooperation may encourage the officer to cite you for a less costly offense instead of what was actually committed. With luck, you might be given only a warning. On the other hand, a belligerent and snarky attitude just makes the situation worse. Moreover, the officer may make a note of your attitude, which won't help your case if you end up going to trial.

Don't admit to anything. If asked whether you know why you were pulled over, reply with a simple and respectful, "No, officer, I do not," even if you do know that you went through a red light or exceeded the speed limit. Don't tell the officer that you're guilty of anything; it's his job to name the offense [I'm using "he" for convenience's sake even though some officers, especially in the traffic division, are female]. There have been instances where a motorist will volunteer that a headlight light is out only to have the officer say that the offense was speeding, but since the driver admitted to another violation, the driver was cited for both violations.

Offer any valid and plausible excuse as simply and honestly as possible. There are no automatic valid excuses, but "I was just at the dentist for root canal work and I don't feel well," "I'm late picking up my child from daycare," or "I'm having that time of the month" may result in just a warning.

Do not—repeat—do not make up farfetched excuses. The Internet is full of supposed examples of evading tickets by lying to officers, but you don't hear about the ones where such lies resulted in ending up in more trouble than would have happened from telling the truth. Remember, too, that any admissions you make can be used against you if the matter goes to court, and justifying preposterous stories in front of a skeptical judge is an exercise in futility . . . and worse.

Let's say that you do receive a ticket. If so, immediately review it for accuracy. If the officer cites you for crossing two lanes of traffic when you only crossed one, ask him to correct the detail. If he chooses not to, make a note of the fact. However, you will not want to call attention to inaccuracies that may help your case, as the citation indicating the wrong license plate number or the wrong time of day.

If you decide to challenge the ticket in court, do not admit guilt. "I was driving only 38 in a 35 mile an hour zone" is an admission of guilt. "I was travel-ing at a safe speed for traffic and road conditions" is not. "I was having lunch with friends, and I for-got about getting back to the parking meter to put in more money" is an admission of guilt. Conversely, "I went back the next day and timed the meter, and it runs fast" is not.

Although it's not an excuse, postponing a court hearing as long as possible can be a good ploy. The officer may forget key details, or he may even be-come unavailable to appear. Often simply showing up in court at any time to challenge a citation may be sufficient. Especially in big cities, there's a good chance that the officer won't appear. And if the offi-cer doesn't, an overworked judge or magistrate may dismiss your case.

In the meantime, if you insist on embroidering or disregarding the truth . . .

Everyone else was speeding, too.

I've been living in Europe, and I thought the speed limit signs were in kilometers.

Excuses for All Occasions

No, I wasn't talking on a cell phone—I was shaving with a portable electric razor.

Sorry, officer, this is the lead car of the Indianapolis 500—I must have taken the wrong turn.

My wife is ovulating, and I'm hurrying home because we want a child.

OFFICER: Where's the fire?
MOTORIST: In your eyes, officer—in your eyes.

I'm running out of gas and I want to get to a gas station in a hurry before I run out.

I just got new tires. They make the car run so smooth that I didn't realize how fast I was going.

I left my glasses at home, and I can't see the speedometer without them.

The Law

Officer, I have a date with a real hottie, and if you saw her, you'd speed, too.

I wanted to see whether my muffler was leaking.

I'm a lawyer, and I'm late for a trial in which I'm defending a state trooper.

Oh, I just pulled out of the car wash. I was blowdrying my car.

The Stones were playing on the radio, and I was keeping the beat to "Jumping Jack Flash."

A motorist in Colorado: I'm from the East. My speedometer is used to sea level and hasn't adjusted to high altitudes.

POLICEMAN: Do you know you're going the wrong way on a oneway street?

MOTORIST: How can I be wrong?—I'm going only one way.

Excuses for All Occasions

TROOPER: I've been waiting for drivers like you all morning.

MOTORIST: Sorry, Officer—I got here as fast as I could. I refuse to acknowledge birthdays anymore, so my license can't possibly be expired.

OFFICER: Your headlights aren't working, Sir—please get out of the car.

MOTORIST: Why, will doing that make them work?

I couldn't signal that turn because my blinker fluid ran out.

TROOPER: Didn't you see the arrow?

DRIVER: Hell, I didn't see the Indian.

The Law

My wife ran off with a state trooper, and when I saw your flashing lights I didn't stop because I thought you might be the trooper trying to bring her back to me.

OFFICER: Did you know you were speeding?

ELDERLY DRIVER: No, I didn't, but thank you for reminding me. [Where upon the driver drove away, leaving the officer scratching his head.]

Traffic Accidents

Again, not the most amusing subject in the world, but the following excuses, again purportedly real, may both delight and instruct. By the way, the advice given for traffic tickets applies here as well.

I don't know how it could have happened. I had one eye on the truck in front, one eye on the pedestrian, and the other on the car behind me.

Going home, I drove into the wrong driveway and hit a tree that I don't have.

The other car collided with mine without giving any warning of its intentions.

I thought the car window was down, but I found out it was up when I put my head through it.

A truck backed through my windshield and into my wife's face.

The Law

A pedestrian hit me and went under my car.

The guy was all over the road. I had to swerve a number of times before I hit him.

I pulled away from the side of the road, glanced over at my mother-in-law, and drove over the embankment.

I swatted at a fly, and I drove into a telephone pole.

When I reached a cross street, a hedge sprang up and obscured my line of vision, and I didn't see the other car.

I had been driving for 40 years when I fell asleep at the wheel and had an accident.

The pedestrian had no idea which way to run, so I ran over him.

I was certain that the old man would never make it to the other side of the street when I hit him.

Excuses for All Occasions

I was on my way to the mechanic with rear end trouble when my universal joint gave way causing me to have an accident.

As I approached an intersection, a sign suddenly appeared in a place where no stop sign had ever appeared before. I was therefore unable to stop in time to avoid the accident.

I struck the pedestrian in order to avoid hitting the bumper of the car in front of me.

My car was legally parked when it backed into the other vehicle.

The indirect cause of the accident was a little guy in a small car with a big mouth.

The telephone pole was approaching. I was attempting to swerve out of its way when it struck the front of my car.

The Law

No one was to blame for the accident but it would never have happened if the other driver had been alert.

When I couldn't avoid a collision, I stepped on the gas and crashed into the other car.

I collided with a stationary truck coming the other way.

I didn't think the speed limit applied after midnight.

Approaching the traffic lights, the car in front suddenly broke.

The accident was caused by me waving to the man I hit last week.

Windshield broke. Cause unknown—probably Voodoo.

None of my witnesses would admit to having seen the mishap until after it happened.

Excuses for All Occasions

I had been learning to drive with power steering. I turned the wheel to what I thought was enough and found myself in a different direction going the opposite way.

The accident happened when the right front door of a car came a round the corner without giving a signal.

I left for work this morning at 7:00 a.m. as usual when I collided straight into a bus. That's because the bus was five minutes early.

An invisible car came out of nowhere, hit my car, and then disappeared.

I was going the wrong way down a one-way street when I hit a car which was not there when going the other way.

I didn't know my foot was still on the accelerator.

The other car shouldn't have been in my way.

The Law

The horse came out of nowhere and landed on my car.

I didn't see the lamppost.

I had to take an important cell phone call.

The car in front of mine had better brakes.

I forgot I was in a parking lot.

I didn't think the railroad used those tracks anymore.

The car didn't come with an instruction manual.

I was picking up my cell phone from the car's floor.

I didn't think the railroad still used those tracks.

Jury Duty

Some people like to serve on juries, whether it's for the fee, it's something to do, it's a way to get out of work, or because they see it as their civic duty. But others don't like it at all and will try to do anything and everything to get off.

Once upon a time just about anyone who didn't want to serve on a state or county court jury could and would be excused just by showing an unwillingness to serve. Moreover, members of certain professions, such as lawyers, doctors, pharmacists, teachers, had automatic exemptions.

Not so any longer, at least in most jurisdictions. In New York State, for example, not only are lawyers eligible, but judges are, too; the state's chief judge sat on a jury several years ago.

What then constitutes a valid excuse to be disqualified from serving?

First of all, anyone over a certain age—70 years old in most jurisdictions—need not serve, although you can if you want to and are otherwise qualified.

Medical reasons are another out, but only those that would preclude your hearing evidence and then making a rational decision.

Then too, perhaps you have an orthopedic condition that prevents you from sitting still for more than 20 minutes at a time, or chronic incontinence that requires frequent trips to the bathroom. Both conditions would prove disruptive to the flow of a trial.

In all medical cases, detailed corroboration from a doctor is essential.[1]

Three groups are exempt from federal jury service and may not serve even if they want to: members of the armed forces on active duty; members of professional fire and police departments; and "public officers" of federal, state, or local governments who

---

1 As for sitting on a federal court jury, you must be a United States citizen at least 18 years of age and reside primarily in the judicial district for one year. You must also be adequately proficient in English, have no disqualifying mental or physical condition, and neither currently be subject to felony charges nor ever have been convicted of a felony (unless your civil rights have been legally restored).

are actively engaged fulltime in the performance of public duties.

You can be excluded in some jurisdictions by showing economic hardship using proof of employment, wage check stubs, and your tax returns as evidence. Owners or operators of small businesses or people who makes a significant amount of income as contractors could claim that they would lose substantial income by not working. It's more difficult if you're salaried, but convincing the judge or county clerk that you can't afford to serve even if you make a fixed income might work on a case-by-case basis.

A single parent who would have to hire someone to pick up the child after school might be able to prove hardship, again on a case-by-case basis.

Excessive knowledge: Let's say that all else fails and you're not disqualified on any of the above grounds. You get your jury duty notice, appear at the appointed time and place, and wait until you're call on a *voir dire*. French for "to see and say" and pronounced "v'wah deer," it's the legal term for the process by which the judge and/or the lawyers interview prospective jurors.

Prospective jurors can be challenged, or excluded, in two ways. A challenge for cause happens when there's a reason why a prospective juror would be biased. You may know one or more parties to the trial or one of the lawyers or even the judge. You may have been involved in a similar civil suit or have been the victim of a crime or lost a relative or friend in a murder. If the lawyers and judge agree that, even though you may try to be impartial, reasons exist that you may not be, you'll be challenged for cause and sent back to the jury room to wait for another *voir dire* panel.

Lawyers have a certain number of preemptory challenges that they can invoke for whatever reason they wish. They need not explain why they don't want a particular person on the case, even if because the person looks . . . well, particular.

You might keep that in mind when you're being examined if you want to be excused. However, remember that judges and lawyers subscribe to the ancient legal doctrine that "no one likes a smart ass" or anyone who makes obvious ploys to get out of serving. That includes sneering at the judicial system, or behaving weird or dumb when your profession would indicate otherwise. Don't bother making such claims as "I could never be fair and impartial," or if a criminal case, "the guy has to be guilty or else the cops wouldn't have arrested him," or if a traffic accident, "all teenage kids are crazy drivers." Judges have heard such assertions many times over, and they know precisely why they're made. Moreover, if you get too cute, you may find yourself fined or imprised for contempt of court.

On the other hand, giving complicated analytical answers to the judge's or lawyers' *voir dire* questions shows that you have a brain in your head and you use it. Lawyers prefer jurors whom they can sway as much if not more so by emotion as by bare facts. If you show that you're your own person, you may not be their cup of tea.

The Law

A handy tool might be the doctrine of jury nullification, which allows juries to return verdicts that are contrary to the letter of the law or the judge's instructions. Courts aren't crazy about the doctrine (judges don't have to tell jurors about it). A little knowledge can be a beneficial thing: letting the judge and lawyers know that you are aware of and believe in jury nullification may result in the opposing lawyers staring first at you, then at each other, and then at the judge, who may well allow a preemptory challenge.

Although it's not exactly "getting out of serving," you can request a postponement either when you receive your jury duty notice or sometimes when you report for service. Some jurisdictions grant one or two automatic postponements and you needn't state the reason. But if you've run out of postponements, yet still can't serve—for example, a sick relative or a business trip you can't avoid—talking to the court clerk or a judge may work. Just be sure you have adequate proof to support your request.

Excuses for All Occasions

Finally, here's an excuse that didn't work:

JUDGE: Is there any reason why you couldn't serve as a juror in this case?

POTENTIAL JUROR: I don't want to be away from my job that long.

JUDGE: Can't they do without you at work?

POTENTIAL JUROR: Yes, but I don't want them to know that.

Some other excuses that didn't work:

I can tell from here—the defendant looks guilty.

I'm a convicted felon.

I believe in capital punishment [useable in civil as well as criminal trials].

The Law

My religion teaches "Judge not that ye be not judged."

The cops wouldn't have arrested the defendant if he wasn't guilty. Cops don't do that.

Excuses (Actual Ones) for Not Filing Tax Returns

It was my accountant's job to file the tax return.

I was depressed.

I meant to mail the return but I left it in my office while away on a business trip.

I refuse to file the tax return on the grounds that it violates my Fifth Amendment rights.

Filing tax returns is against my religious beliefs.

I am exempt from the Federal income tax because I am an African-American.

The Law

The Paperwork Reduction Act relieves Americans of their duty to file tax returns.

I was not required to file my tax return because I never received a court order to do so.

Payment of the income tax is voluntary.

The Internal Revenue Code does not apply outside of the District of Columbia.

I relied upon my prior tax representatives, and they gave me bad advice.

I am not liable for the Federal income tax because I am a Native Hawaiian.

We filed our tax return late because I am a C.P.A. and I was too busy preparing other people's tax returns to file my own tax return on time.

Social Security taxes were already withheld from my paycheck by my employer, so I am excused from paying income taxes on the same wages because that would be double taxation.

The harassment at work exacerbated my stress-related medical problems, which necessitated my going out on disability leave, which compounded my misdiagnosed and untreated learning disabilities and caused me to have no income so I couldn't pay my property taxes.

As a citizen, I have the right to work without the taxation of my labor.

I was convicted and imprisoned for not filing my 1987, 1988, 1989, and 1990 Federal income tax returns, and after my release from prison I had difficulty compiling my records so I didn't file my 1993, 1994, and 1995 Oregon state income tax returns

The Law

I have an obsessive compulsive disorder which caused me to hoard every piece of paper and object with which I came in contact, so my husband and I were too disorganized to file our tax returns on time.

When I was audited by the IRS many years ago, the agent told me that he had never seen a taxpayer as scrupulous and honest in his affairs as me, and that I would never have to file a tax return again.

We didn't pay our part of our Massachusetts state income tax on time because we intended to pay it the next year so we could get a deduction on our Federal income tax return the next year.

I didn't pay my State income taxes because a New York State Department of Labor employee told me that the criminal charges against me and my company for not paying wages and benefits to the employees would be dropped if I turned over all available cash to the Department of Labor to pay the employees.

I was involved in a commercial dispute in which the court made a bad decision against me, and I asked the Minnesota Attorney General's Office to help me get the bad court decision reversed but they refused to get involved, so I didn't pay my Minnesota state income taxes because the Government of Minnesota did not give me the protection I deserve.

I agreed that I owed $185,349.79 in back New York State income taxes for the purposes of my plea bargain to avoid jail time for filing false tax returns, but I really owed only $72,266.00, and I should be refunded the additional which I already paid in restitution as part of my plea bargain.

The Law

I didn't file my income tax returns for 1987 or 1988 because I was afraid that doing so would draw attention to the fact that I had not filed for 1986.

I was a Federal parolee at the time I earned the income, and am now incarcerated by the State of Oregon. Federal law provides that Federal parolees are in the legal custody and under the control of the U.S. Attorney General, so therefore, the Attorney General should be liable for the tax on the income I earned.

Our church refuses to withhold employee employment taxes because we believe that it is a sin to accept the authority of secular worldly governments.

My cousin really owned the store and I never worked there, but I let him put the business in my name because my cousin was an illegal immigrant with an arrest record, and after my cousin was killed in a robbery attempt the business tax returns were never filed or paid.

I claimed a total exemption from payroll tax withholding because I had lost a lot of money gambling and had to pay large sums of money to loan sharks every week.

I was diagnosed as suffering from hypertension, diabetes, and obesity.

I didn't file my 1992 tax returns because my wife refused to give me my son's social security number so that I could claim him as a dependant. I didn't file my 1993 or 1994 tax returns due to marital discord.

The bookkeeper was injured in an accident and couldn't work, and I also was injured in an accident and then became pregnant so I couldn't work, and when I came back to work the computer system had crashed so the records were lost.

The Law

After I moved from Utah to New Jersey, I asked someone in New Jersey about my Utah income tax, and was told that the tax I owed Utah was so small that it wasn't worth worrying about, so I just said, "Hell with it!"

I attribute my tax filing failures to my stupidity and to the fees I owed to my tax accountant at the time.

I did not file my state income tax returns for the years 1992 through 1998 because I believed that I would not receive a refund big enough to make it worth the time to file.

I didn't file our joint income tax return on time because I was waiting for my husband to be released from prison, and they kept him longer than I had expected.

I read a book called <u>Vultures in Eagles Clothing</u> and, having read the book, developed the belief that I was not subject to the Virginia state income tax.

I went to a lonely road and prayed that I should become self-sufficient and be able to help others, and a short time later I received a $836,939.19 check upon my discharge from the Army. I didn't report it on my tax return because I thought the check was a miraculous answer to my prayer instead of a Government error.

I stopped filing my income tax returns in 1990 after my mother gave me a videotape which said that the Internal Revenue Code did not specifically require people to file tax returns or pay income taxes.

I defer to my wife on financial matters because her income is greater than mine, but she has a tendency to go off on spending binges, and I wasn't strong enough to make her pay the taxes.

The Law

I led a double life. In my public life as barrister, community and family man, I achieved the highest possible standards that I was capable of, but in my private persona I became increasingly burnt out and drawn towards deliberate ignorance and recklessness as to the risks and consequences of understating income on my tax returns.

We didn't know that we were required to report the money we embezzled as income on our tax returns.

I voluntarily opted out of the Federal tax system so that I could do more for my community, my fiancée, my country, and the State of North Dakota.

. . . And finally, Leona Helmsley, the hotel-owning "Queen of Mean" who was convicted of tax evasion reportedly said, "We don't pay taxes. Only the little people pay taxes."

"If you don't want to do something, one excuse is as good as another."

—*Yiddish Proverb*

8.

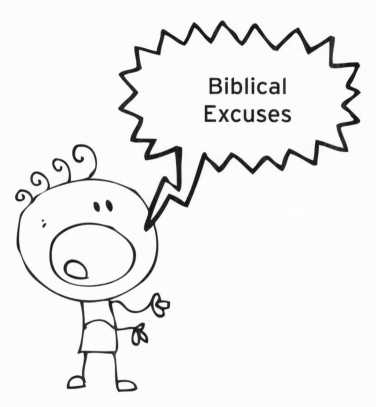

The man [Adam] said, "The woman whom you gave to be with me, she gave me fruit of the tree, and I ate." Then the Lord God said to the woman, "What is this that you have done?" The woman said, "The serpent deceived me, and I ate."

Genesis 3:1213

And the Lord said unto Cain, "Where is Abel, thy brother?" And he said, "I know not: Am I my brother's keeper?"

Genesis 4:9

But Moses said to the Lord, "Oh, my Lord, I am not eloquent, either in the past or since you have spoken to your servant, but I am slow of speech and of tongue." Then the Lord said to him, "Who has made man's mouth? Who makes him mute, or deaf, or seeing, or blind? Is it not I, the Lord?

Biblical Excuses

Now therefore go, and I will be with your mouth and teach you what you shall speak." But he said, "Oh, my Lord, please send someone else." Then the anger of the Lord was kindled against Moses and he said, "Is there not Aaron, your brother, the Levite? I know that he can speak well. Behold, he is coming out to meet you, and when he sees you, he will be glad in his heart."

Exodus 4:1014

And Aaron said, "Let not the anger of my Lord burn hot. You know the people, that they are set on evil. For they said to me, 'Make us gods who shall go before us. As for this Moses, the man who brought us up out of the land of Egypt, we do not know what has become of him.' So I said to them, 'Let any who have gold take it off.' So they gave it to me, and I threw it into the fire, and out came this calf."

Exodus 32:2224

Excuses for All Occasions

And the angel of the Lord appeared to him and said to him, "The Lord is with you, O mighty man of valor." And Gideon said to him, "Please, sir, if the Lord is with us, why then has all this happened to us? And where are all his wonderful deeds that our fathers recounted to us, saying, 'Did not the Lord bring us up from Egypt?' But now the Lord has forsaken us and given us into the hand of Midian." And the Lord turned to him and said, "Go in this might of yours and save Israel from the hand of Midian; do not I send you?" And he said to him, "Please, Lord, how can I save Israel? Behold, my clan is the weakest in Manasseh, and I am the least in my father's house." And the Lord said to him, "But I will be with you, and you shall strike the Midianites as one man. . . ."

Judges 6:12-17

Now the word of the Lord came to me, saying, "Before I formed you in the womb I knew you, and before you were born I consecrated you; I appointed you a prophet to the nations." Then I said, "Ah, Lord God! Behold, I do not know how to speak, for I am only a youth." But the Lord said to me, "Do not say, 'I am only a youth'; for to all to whom I send you, you shall go, and whatever I command you, you shall speak."

Jeremiah 1:410

To another he said, "Follow me." But he said, "Lord, let me first go and bury my father." And Jesus said to him, "Leave the dead to bury their own dead. But as for you, go and proclaim the kingdom of God." Yet another said, "I will follow you, Lord, but let me first say farewell to those at my home." Jesus said to him, "No one who puts his hand to the plow and looks back is fit for the kingdom of God."

Luke 9:5962

Excuses for All Occasions

But they all alike began to make excuses. The first said to him, "I have bought a field, and I must go out and see it. Please have me excused." And another said, "I have bought five yoke of oxen, and I go to examine them. Please have me excused." And another said, "I have married a wife, and therefore I cannot come."

Luke 14:1820

Therefore you have no excuse, O man, every one of you who judges. For in passing judgment on another you condemn yourself, because you, the judge, practice the very same things. We know that the judgment of God rightly falls on those who practice such things. Do you suppose, O man—you who judge those who practice such things and yet do them yourself—that you will escape the judgment of God? Or do you presume on the riches of his kindness and forbearance and patience, not knowing that God's kindness is meant to lead you to repentance? But because of your hard and impenitent heart, you are storing up wrath for yourself on the day of wrath when God's righteous judgment will be revealed. . . .

Romans 2:129

And as he reasoned about righteousness and self-control and the coming judgment, Felix was alarmed and said, "Go away for the present. When I get an opportunity I will summon you."

Acts 24:25

"Several excuses are always less convincing than one."

—*Aldous Huxley*

9.

All right, boys and girls and children of all ages, you did something you shouldn't have or you didn't do something you should have. And you've been caught red-handed or, if not, the circumstantial evidence is overwhelming.

Kids learn, and at an early age, Life Lesson #1: make an excuse, and they perfect their skill throughout their lives. Here are some tried-and- often-true ones (not that they always work, but they're tried-and-often-true). And if they're not true, as the man said, never let a good story stand between you and the truth.

Adults will find more than a few here that'll work for them too.

She started.

No, he started.

It wasn't me.

I was going to do it before you asked me to.

It's not my turn.

Kids' Excuses

What list?

I lost the list.

I didn't break the vase—it just came down.

Don't ever call my room a mess—it's a work of art.

I forgot.

I can't let Aunt Mary kiss me—she smells funny.

That box of Oreos came without the creamy filling.

I didn't do it of my own free will—my brother hypnotized me to do it.

My evil twin did it.

MOTHER: Clean your room.
CHILD: I can't find it through all the mess.

Excuses for All Occasions

The dog ate your birthday cake, Mom.

My elbows aren't on the table—I'm holding them three inches above it.

What do you expect from me, Dad—remember, I'm just a little kid.

I did it last time.

I thought it was my brother's turn.

But you don't understand—none of my friends have bedtimes. Their parents let them stay up as long as they like.

I was going to bring home my report card, but some big kids took it out of my backpack and started playing monkey-in-the-middle, and then a dog grabbed it and chewed it up. Honest!

No, our teacher never gives us homework on weekends.

Kids' Excuses

I'm not playing with my food—this is home-work for art class.

It's too late to start that chore now. I'll do it tomorrow—first thing.

All my friends' parents pay them to do chores.

I don't know how.

Let's wait till this TV show is over—it's my favorite.

I would have cleaned up my room, but while I was making my bed, I fell on it and the next thing I knew, I woke up.

This video game was a class assignment. The score will count on my grade, so please don't distract me.

I can't hang up my clothes—there's a scary ghost in my closet.

Excuses for All Occasions

I can't go to sleep—there's a boogieman under my bed.

You can't be mad at me for doing that. You gotta love me . . . I'm the baby of the family.

You're right, Mom. I'm wrong. Please don't hate me.

CHILD: Mom, would you punish me for something I didn't do?
MOTHER: Of course not.
CHILD: That's good because I didn't clean my room like you told me to.

The leaves are too wet to rake.

The lawn is too wet to mow.

The snow is too wet to shovel.

I'll wait till the snow stops—then I'll shovel the driveway.

Kids' Excuses

The garage is too dirty to clean.

Why should I clean up after the dog? He made the mess.

I was looking after my brother like you told me to, but when I looked away for a minute, aliens from space abducted him.

He started.

I didn't make my bed because I'm going to sleep in it tonight and it'll get messed up again.

I can't—I have a stomach ache. You know how sensitive my stomach is.

You never told me to.

I didn't break that vase on the mantle that had Grandpa's ashes in it—he must have wanted to get out.

The cat got into the refrigerator and ate all the cupcakes.

Excuses for All Occasions

It was like that all the time, I swear it was!

My brother could do that faster and better than I can.

Spinach makes me break out.

MOTHER: Pick up your room.
CHILD: It's too heavy.

I can't eat my broccoli. There were people at the mall giving out free samples of food, and I ate too much. [pause] What's that you say you have for dessert?

I didn't brush my teeth because I wanted to save water.

We can't leave yet! I can't go without either my lucky rubber pig or a piece of string!

10.

Having an Overweight Dog or Cat

Fido/Fluffy is always hungry.

All my other pets have lived to ripe old ages.

Fido is old, and I want him to live the rest of his life fat and happy.

Fluffy will suffer from malnutrition.

Fido hates going out to exercise.

Fluffy's only pleasure is eating and sleeping.

It's the breed.

But it's a small bowl/dish—I have to keep refilling it.

Fido's/Fluffy's parents were on the heavy side, so it must be genetic.

Everybody in the family feeds Fido/Fluffy.

Excuses for Leaving a Dinner or a Party Early

I'm sure it's not your cooking, but I suddenly don't feel so well.

I've got an early tee time/tennis match/fishing trip tomorrow.

I thought I'd gotten over it, but I'm still uncomfortable being at the same gathering as my ex.

Didn't I tell you that I have another party to go to after this one?

The babysitter says she has a big test tomorrow.

I flew home yesterday, and jet lag is getting to me.

Ow! my tooth. I'd better see a dentist right away.

I've a long drive home, and besides, the weather forecast calls for snow/ice/hurricane.

I have a sales report to finish for the morning.

We've an early flight/train to catch.

The Ebay auction for a set of golf clubs that I want ends in an hour, and I want to be home for it.

Our dog's bladder isn't what it once was.

My husband is allergic to your cat.

The only day that the mechanic can work on my car is tomorrow, and it'll be an all-day job.

That's the most bigoted remark I ever heard—I'm leaving!

Excuses to Stay on the Computer (or Smart Phone)

I need a file for my homework, and it's taking forever to download. I'm playing this video game just to kill time.

cant u c im tweeting!

I've got to get even on Texas Hold'em.

I'm . . . um, deleting spam. That's right—spam.

This neighborhood is so slow—my phone reception gets only one bar. Where are we, Mongolia?

The tech guy put me on hold—he's looking something up. In the meantime, I'm just killing time.

The Ebay auction closes in 20 minutes.

Excuses for All Occasions

Everybody's waiting for my next blog.

Wikipedia can't answer my question, and I'm sure it'll be on the test tomorrow, so I have to keep looking.

I don't know how the widow of an Ethiopian billionaire prince found me, but she has a sure-fire business deal she wants me to represent her on.

That blonde on *College Girls On Spring Break* looks a lot like your brother's younger daughter. I'd better keep watching to make sure it isn't her.

I need a black seven to go on that red eight.

I'm closing in on getting 500 Facebook friends.

I'm buying you a present.

Travel Excuses

Airline pilots to passengers:

Ladies and gentlemen, we have a broken fuel pump and it is going to take too long to fix it so we are going to take off anyway. Don't worry. On this aircraft we can transfer fuel from one tank to another so we don't actually need the pump. Anyway, if that doesn't work we will just have to land in Seattle on the way to refuel . . . Hold on, we want be able to land there as we won't have burnt enough fuel, and this plane has a maximum landing weight. We will have to fly a bit farther, but we will worry about that once we are airborne.

We are canceling all our flights today because our flight systems are down.

We will be delayed because the copilot can't find his pilot certificate.

Excuses for All Occasions

Flight cancelled due to potential weather problems.

We'll have to shift all passengers to seats in the rear of the plane because the rear luggage hold door won't open and we need to balance the load for takeoff.

We missed our turn on the takeoff line, but don't worry, we'll make up the time in the air.

The plane is late in leaving because we're waiting for 30 connecting Panamanians.

The crew is giving a birthday party to one of the flight attendants.

The lavatory is broken because someone tried to flush a bag of pot.

Flight delayed because the First Officer misplaced his medical certificate.

We're sorry for the delay, but we're having some problems loading the cheetah.

The ground crew rammed the plane with the tug.

[On Alitalia] The plane, she is not well.

[From the airline to a sleeping passenger who wasn't awakened when the flight reached its destination and who awoke to find the plane was in a hanger] Although there was no excuse for the incident that occurred, it appears the flight attendant on this occasion was dealing with several wheelchair passengers and coordinating their departure from the aircraft.

Although the flight attendant advised he did look back into the aircraft to check for any passengers still on board, he did not walk through the aircraft cabin as he was engaged with handling the passengers in wheelchairs requiring assistance.

I can assure you that no previous incident of this nature has occurred and that this matter has been thoroughly reviewed with the crew member concerned and other crews operating similar aircraft to ensure an incident of this type does not happen again.

Please accept our sincere apologies for the inconvenience caused to you on this occasion.

Rental Car Damage Excuses:

I don't normally drive like a crazy person, but it wasn't like I own the car.

[From a man who, dressed as a woman, returned a damaged car] I wasn't used to wearing high heels.

It's your car . . . you pay the traffic tickets.

Even More Excuses for Even More Occasions

We were attacked by monkeys.

I thought I could damage the car since I had paid the deposit.

It's the rock's fault it got in the way.

The road was too narrow, and we ran into a sheep.

The heater wasn't working properly. It was stuck on 'high,' and that melted my shoes.

"And oftentimes excusing of a fault / Doth make the fault the worse by the excuse."

—*William Shakespeare, King John, Act IV, Scene 2*

11.

Words to the Wise . . . and Wiseguys: Quotations and Proverbs about Excuses

"I never knew a man who was good at making excuses who was good at anything else."

—Benjamin Franklin

"The real man is one who always finds excuses for others, but never excuses himself."

—Henry Ward Beecher

"For many people, an excuse is better than an achievement because an achievement, no matter how great, leaves you having to prove yourself again in the future, but an excuse can last for life."

—Eric Hoffer

Words to the Wise . . . and Wiseguys

"He who excuses himself accuses himself."

—French proverb

"People with integrity do what they say they are going to do. Others have excuses."

—Laura Schlessinger

"An excuse is worse and more terrible than a lie; for an excuse is a lie guarded."

—Alexander Pope

"Excuses are the nails used to build a house of failure."

—Don Wilder

Excuses for All Occasions

"The only man who is really free is the one who can turn down an invitation to dinner without giving an excuse."

—Jules Renard

"Ninety-nine percent of the failures come from people who have the habit of making excuses."

—George Washington Carver

"Don't make excuses, make good."

—L. Ron Hubbard

"It is wise to focus your energies on answers, not excuses."

—Anonymous

"Difficulty is the excuse history never accepts."

—*Edward R. Murrow*

"Apology is only egotism the wrong side out."

—*Oliver Wendell Holmes*

"Two wrongs don't make a right, but they make a good excuse."

—*Thomas Szasz*

"The streets of the City of Failure are paved with alibis some of which are absolutely perfect."

—*Harry A. Earnshaw,*

Excuses for All Occasions

"Success is a tale of obstacles overcome, and for every obstacle overcome, an excuse not used."

—Robert Brault

"Maybe you don't like your job, maybe you didn't get enough sleep. Well nobody likes their job, nobody got enough sleep. Maybe you just had the worst day of your life, but you know, there's no escape, there's no excuse, so just suck it up and be nice."

—Ani Difranco

"How strange to use 'You only live once'" as an excuse to throw it away."

—Bill Copeland

Words to the Wise . . . and Wiseguys

"Don't do what you'll have to find an excuse for."

—English Proverb

"I attribute my success to this: I never gave or took an excuse. "

—Florence Nightingale

"Excuses are the tools with which persons with no purpose in view build for themselves great monuments of nothing."

—Steven Graham

"Hold yourself responsible for a higher standard than anyone else expects of you. Never excuse yourself."

—Henry Ward Beecher

Excuses for All Occasions

"We excuse our sloth under the pretext of difficulty."

—Marcus Fabius Quintilian

"There is no such thing as a list of reasons. There is either one sufficient reason or a list of excuses."

—Robert Brault

"We have more ability than will power, and it is often an excuse to ourselves that we imagine that things are impossible."

—François de la Rochefoucauld

Words to the Wise . . . and Wiseguys

"We weave our excuses around events."

—Phillip Pulfrey

"Destiny: A tyrant's authority for crime and a fool's excuse for failure."

—Ambrose Bierce

"He who cannot dance claims the floor is uneven."

—Hindu proverb

"No doubt Jack the Ripper excused himself on the grounds that it was human nature."

—A.A. Milne

Excuses for All Occasions

"Bad men excuse their faults; good men abandon them."

—*Anonymous*

"It is wise to direct your anger towards problems, not people; to focus your energies on answers, not excuses."

—*William Arthur Ward*

"Any excuse will serve a tyrant."

—*Aesop's Fables ["The Wolf and The Lamb"]*

"The absent are never without fault, nor the present without excuse."

—*Benjamin Franklin*

Words to the Wise . . . and Wiseguys

"It's so easy to make excuses. Even professional writers have days when they'd rather clean the toilet than do the writing."

—Octavia Butler

"Don't make excuses and don't talk about it. Do it."

—Melvyn Douglas

"Excuses change nothing, but make everyone feel better."

—Mason Cooley

"I am not the kind of woman who excuses her mistakes while reminding us of what used to be."

—*Gene Tierney*

"I do not believe in excuses. I believe in hard work as the prime solvent of life's problems."

—*James Cash Penney*

"I'm not going to say that every record I've put out was the greatest record in history, but I'd stand by even the bad ones. Don't make excuses, make hits."

—*Pete Waterman*

Words to the Wise . . . and Wiseguys

"If you really want to do it, you do it. There are no excuses."

—*Bruce Nauman*

"It happens to the best of them. You lay off singing and your throat gets out of practice. No excuses. I blew it."

—*Bobby Darin*

"Not managing your time and making excuses are two bad habits. Don't put them both together by claiming you 'don't have the time.'"

—*Bo Bennett*

"People spend too much time finding other people to blame, too much energy finding excuses for not being what they are capable of being, and not enough energy putting themselves on the line, growing out of the past, and getting on with their lives."

—*J. Michael Straczynski*

"People want a copout Listen, I'm a realist, and I talk about motivation, talk about all the things it takes to be greater or are important to win and people want to use excuses all the time."

—*Mike Ditka*

Words to the Wise . . . and Wiseguys

"The best job goes to the person who can get it done without passing the buck or coming back with excuses."

—G. M. Trevelyan

"The trick is not how much pain you feel but how much joy you feel. Any idiot can feel pain. Life is full of excuses to feel pain, excuses not to live, excuses, excuses, excuses."

—Erica Jong

"There aren't nearly enough crutches in the world for all the lame excuses."

—Marcus Stroup

"I will not take "but" for an answer."

—Langston Hughes

"The best job goes to the person who can get it done without passing the buck or coming back with excuses."

—Napoleon Hill

"Sometimes, people use age as a convenient excuse. Other people, though, go on to achieve their greatest accomplishments in life in later years."

—Catherine Pulsifer

Words to the Wise . . . and Wiseguys

"Don't look for excuses to lose. Look for excuses to win."

—*Chi Chi Rodriguez*

"Whoever wants to be a judge of human nature should study people's excuses."

—*Christian Friedrich Hebbel*

"Your letter of excuses has arrived. I receive the letter but do not admit the excuses except in courtesy, as when a man treads on your toes and begs your pardon the pardon is granted, but the joint aches, especially if there is a corn upon it."

—*Lord Byron*

"Justifying a fault doubles it."

—French Proverb

"The day you take complete responsibility for yourself, the day you stop making any excuses, that's the day you start to the top."

—O. J. Simpson